LOYALTIES

VONTEZ

DESTINY'S PUBLICATIONS

LOYALTIES

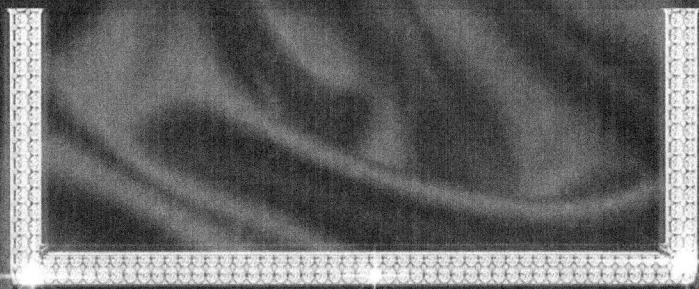

VONTEZ

DESTINY'S
PUBLICATIONS

Destiny's Publications
P.O. Box 24362
Cincinnati, OH 45224-9998

First Destiny's Publications trade paperback edition June 2016

Cover design: Consandra Wright

10 9 8 7 6 5 4 3 2 1

Manufactured in the United States of America

Dedication

This book is dedicated to my family and friends for their unrelenting support of my dreams. Especially my Aunt Johnnie Mae who encouraged me to write! Without you this book would not have come to fruition.

I also give thanks to my supporters who have passed on, starting with my Mother, Barbara Lee Jackson, my first friend, Anthony Paul Owens and my dear friend,

Reggie "Big Reg" Spiller.

Chapter 1

It was a crisp, cool, late, fall morning and Verdale was on I-70 East, in his custom Pearl White 2014 Cadillac Escalade with Lexani Rims and 22" inch Vogue tires, heading to one of the many Ohio state penitentiaries to see his older brother Vontez. Vontez was only 16 months deep into a 4 year bid he had received for cocaine trafficking in Cincinnati, a.k.a Snitchanati; a nickname given to the city by visiting connects, who were told on by a bunch of mid-level hustlas, who couldn't hold water if they were a 50 gallon fish tank. The charges against Vontez were acquired no differently, being told on by an appropriately named dude "Snake", someone he had dealt with for close to seven years in the game.

Facing two, felony one charges that carried 3 to 10 years each, Vontez, with the thoroughness of gangstas past, accepted the four year plea deal worked out by his crafty attorney and the Regional Narcotics Unit (RENU), the arresting agency on the case. Vontez knew that if Snake had taken the witness stand against him, he would have undoubtedly received the maximum sentence.

Verdale, while riding in the luxury of his newly purchased SUV, listening to the UGK classic, 'Hi Life', received a phone call on his Samsung Galaxy S5 that was synced to his car stereo system. The monitor screen flashed "Moms", without hesitation, he hit the answer button.

"Good morning Mama," he greeted her.

"Good morning son, even though in five more minutes it will be noon," she replied with motherly sarcasm that over the years he had grown to love.

"How far are you away? You know that you have to be there by 12:30 for a one o'clock visit since it's a half-hour processing time. And you know how your big brother is, like a broke doctor on a Sunday – he ain't got no patience," she joked and they shared a laugh.

"I just passed the 40 mile marker to Caldwell, Ohio Ma. I should be there right on schedule," he replied. "Did you get that money I left on the mantle for you?" he asked.

"I sure did and thank you son, you know that you don't have to do that all of the time. I'm perfectly capable of taking care of myself, after all, I did raise you and your brother off this city worker's income, but you know I really appreciate it," his mother says.

"I know you do Ma. I just want you to have all of the finer things and be able to keep up on the house maintenance," Verdale said with a smile.

"What, you want me to get a butler or something with the amount you leave me every time!" she joked again. "But really, I do appreciate you and your brother fo'real. Although I'm not totally happy with your lifestyle, I am proud of the responsible family oriented men that you two have grown to be. Tell your brother that I love him and to call me on Sunday, after four o'clock. I'll be home from church by then and you know I love you too Babyboy."

"I love you too Mama," Verdale replied back in a boyish tone. He couldn't help but feel childlike every time she called him Babyboy.

"When you *gonna* bring my grandkids to see me? I know the twins are growing like wildflowers," Mama said with a wit that only she possessed.

"Maybe after church on Sunday, when you get home. I'll see if Gina feels like making some of her famous German chocolate cake and I'll pick up a bucket of Kentucky Fried Chicken and some sides. That is if you feel like eating Sunday dinner with us Ma?" Verdale wisecracks.

"Ooh, you know how I love that girl's chocolate cake! I'll see y'all around 4 o'clock on Sunday then Babyboy," Valencia states.

"Ok, Ma. I love you!"

"I love you too son and you be safe!"

"I will!" Verdale said with a smile on his face as he and his mother said their goodbyes.

As he passed by the 10 mile marker for the Caldwell exit that would take him to the prison that housed his older brother, Verdale reflected on his childhood. Rather the childhood he and his brother shared, being raised by an independent strong black woman. Qualities that he so strongly admired in his mother, Valencia. He had seen her make numerous sacrifices in her life for him and his brother.

The times she went without buying herself new summer dresses in order to be able to lace him and his brother with the latest fashions for their back-to-school gear. How she continued to sacrifice after school had begun, in order to make sure they were all smiles on Christmas morning. Verdale also thought about the many number of unseen sacrifices that she must have made in order for him and his brother to be involved in the sports activities, in which they excelled. How she had taken the time to make her boys self-sufficient, by teaching them how to wash and fold clothes, clean and cook for themselves and the importance of a good education. Verdale and Vontez, despite their street affiliation, both attended and graduated from 4 year universities. Both had received athletic scholarships. Vontez played cornerback for Bowling Green University and Verdale received a track and field scholarship from the University of Toledo.

He thought about how she had been a mother and father to them, after their father had been killed in an after-hours spot when the boys were 6 and 3 years old. Now, 30 years later and a parent himself, Verdale realized that his mother was one-hell-of-a-woman, to so courageously take on the burden of raising two young boys to manhood, and doing it in such grand style. During his moments of introspection Verdale nearly missed his exit. As he got over two lanes, in order to reach the off-ramp, he noticed that the state troopers had a semi-truck pulled over. He said to himself, "I hope that wasn't nobody's pack in there."

As he got off the exit and made a right-hand turn he couldn't help but to take in the beauty and isolation of the country scenery. The leaves had begun to turn into a fall spectacle of colors. The vivid red, orange and yellow-brown leaves were like something out of a movie, or better yet, like a landscape portrait painted by Bob Ross, the white guy with an Afro on PBS. As Verdale made a right-hand turn into the prison complex, the beauty of the landscape was rudely interrupted by the drab grey buildings of the Noble Correctional Facility.

An uneasiness overcame him as always, when he set foot on the new age plantation soil. Because of his own extracurricular activities, he knew that one day this could be his own fate. But he was in too deep now and he would at least have to hold it down until his brother returned to take back the crown of the streets, which he once held. Once Vontez had been set up, Verdale, who had a very lucrative janitorial business as well as a few investment properties felt compelled to substitute for his brother since he was the one who had turned him on to "*the connect*".

Verdale had met Fernando a.k.a. "Flash", so named because of his blazing speed while they both ran track at Toledo. Fernando, because of his grades, had been overlooked by some of the major Division 1 Schools from his own home state of California, and had gratefully accepted the full-ride that Toledo offered him.

Verdale who had fell back on *hustlin'* once he entered college, had instantly saw dollar signs and the profit margin that he and his brother could make when Flash told him the prices of the werk back home.

Verdale knew his older brother was still *trappin'* hard, while in school, after football season of course. He decided to tell his brother about the newfound plug that he had coincidentally ran into, while on the track team. After Verdale had connected the dots, so to speak, his *brother* told him to continue to fall back and he would give him a grand a week just for hooking things up.

Verdale, being a business major in college, had managed to save up over $160,000 before he graduated; just 3 and 1/2 years after the first deal went down. That enabled him to start a janitorial company once he completed college and fund his first three rental property investments. Vontez, who was definitely no slouch himself when it came to having a business mind, invested in the Barber and Beauty industry. What started off with one small Barber and Beauty shop blossomed into a chain of 12 shops throughout the Midwest;

branded, "Urban Styles Barber and Beauty", with each shop having a very lucrative hair store on the premises.

In addition to the Barber and Beauty Shops & Hair Stores, after graduation Vontez started a sports management company using two of his closest friends, Bernard Spiller and Louis Malone from the football team as the front men. The name of the sports management company was "MBK" Sports Management. The MBK standing for "My Brother's Keeper", something that the three men were extremely proud of and stood by. They had seen a number of teammates and opponents taken advantage of by greedy sports agents that did not have their clients' best interest at heart.

Verdale parked his stylish luxury SUV in the far end of the prison parking lot, as he always did, to avoid any inadvertent dings that neighboring cars might 'cause. He made sure to check his surroundings, as usual, to make sure no eyes were watching him as he emptied his pockets of their contents and took off his jewelry. He wore a three carat pinky ring on his right hand, a two carat platinum wedding ring on his left hand, a 30-inch platinum rope chain, with a five carat iced out cross on the end and a one carat VVS clarity earring in his left ear, which was the only piece of jewelry he left on. He wore a white on white Adidas sweat suit, a white tee and some white on white shell toe Adidas shoes, and as simple as his attire was, Verdale looked like money!

Maybe it was his "Puffy" like swagger when he walked...his head held proudly and shoulders back. His mother always told him that a man of distinction had a certain posture that commanded respect. Verdale grabbed 50 singles and placed them in a quart sized plastic bag and hit the alarm button on his Cadillac's remote key fob.

The tower guard instantly recognized the walk of Verdale; he had seen it for nearly a year and a half from Vontez when he walked the track on the yard, the prison yard. Verdale dreaded the emasculating process that awaited him in order to see his older brother. He signed in then walked through a metal detector. Then he was patted down very thoroughly by a guard, who seemed to enjoy that part of his job way too much. At first he mean-mugged the guard once he was done patting him down, as if to challenge him. He forced himself to smile and nod his head at the obviously racist guard who couldn't do anything to him, but could make things tougher on his older brother.

"Mr. Lewis sit at table eight", the more personable of the visitation guards said.

"Thank you sir and have a blessed day," Verdale replied.

Verdale walked over to table number eight, thankful that the table was at the end of the row, so he and his brother could have a little bit of privacy and wouldn't be sandwiched in between two other sets of visitors. That was something that they both hated with a passion, other inmates *ear hustlin'* their conversations. Whether they were talking about family matters or business, both men shared the commonality of being private.

After waiting about five minutes without seeing his brother emerge from the door in which the inmates entered the room, Verdale went to the vending machine and purchased two packs of chicken wings, a salad with ranch dressing and a 20 ounce Dr. Pepper for his brother, knowing his order with great familiarity. He ordered a turkey club sandwich and iced tea for himself. While putting the two packs of chicken wings in the microwave, Vontez appeared in the doorway looking more like an NFL running back than the cornerback he played in college.

He wore a close cropped taper and a goatee that stood out against his caramel complexion. He was a chiseled 5'10", 225lb charismatic man, whose mere presence commanded respect. He nodded to his brother and took a seat at table number eight.

When Verdale returned to the table with wings, salad, sandwich and beverages in hand, he sat them down on the table and his brother stood up. They shared a brotherly embrace before sitting down together.

"What's up *Bruh Bruh*?" Vontez said starting off the conversation. "You're looking good as always. How are Gina and the kids?"

"Everybody's good! The kids are getting so big and Gina sends her love. But look at you all swole and stuff! Do y'all have weights in here or something?" Verdale jokes with a smile and chuckle.

"Naw, ain't no weights, *Bruh*. Just the pull-up and dip bars and *hella* push-ups!" Vontez said with jovialness in his voice.

"Well damn! You in here looking like Herschel Walker or somebody. I might have to get you an agent and sign you up for special-teams or something," he joked with his brother.

"Boy you still crazy like Mama! How is Mama doing anyway?" Vontez asked.

"She doing well. She wants you to call her around 4 o'clock on Sunday after she gets home from church. Me, Gina and the kids will be there too. We're bringing some KFC over to eat Sunday dinner with her," Verdale said.

"That's what's up Lil *Bruh*. I'll call as soon as count clears. We got 4 o'clock count, so it will be closer to 4:30pm when I can call. I'm happy that you're still staying close with Moms, Lil *Bruh*. I know she's upset about some of my life choices," Vontez said with seriousness in his voice.

"Well yeah, she's not happy about the lifestyle we partake in, but she still loves us, no less," Verdale said in response.

"Any word on the whereabouts of that nigga, Snake?" asked Vontez.

"Yeah, *Bruh*, you already know that I'm on it! Word has it this nigga is only right down the road in Louisville!" Verdale quickly replies.

"Word!" an inquisitive Vontez says.

"Word *Bruh*, he's got a hole-in-da-wall club, on the Westside, but we already got a couple of girls in there working", a confident Verdale says.

"Oh yeah, I see the gangster *startin'* to come out in you Lil Dale," Vontez jokingly stated. (No matter how grown they were, he was always going to look at Verdale as his kid brother; Even though he stood 6ft tall and weighed around 190 lbs., slim but muscular, in the fashion of a Usain Bolt type of way.)

"Naw, *Bruh*, it ain't that I'm trying to be *gangsta* or nothin', but you know I live by the motto "Loyalty is Royalty", just like you. And the underhanded, disloyal and not to mention shiesty-ass shit that Snake pulled, has to be dealt with, point blank! For two simple reasons in my book; one being that the nigga snitched and bit the hand that was feeding his lame-ass, and two being that we have to set an example that you don't fuck with us and get away with it! They need to know that there's some consequences and repercussions behind that shit!" Verdale boldly stated to his brother.

"See that's what I'm *talkin'* *'bout* Lil *Bruh*. I knew you could hold it down! Just make sure you keep your hands clean and get E-Tone and J. J for the dirty work. That's what we got a goon-squad for. Shit, the way you sounding up in here, sound like you want to box this nigga *yo'* damn self!" Vontez said excitedly in a playful manner. The brothers shared a laugh and bumped fists.

"*Bruh*, you crazy! I just get hyped thinking about that shit! Niggas just don't know how deep shit can get when you fuck wit the wrong one. I'll put a bitch on a nigga and she'll fuck his ass until he pass out, then cut that nigga's throat the same night!" Verdale said with a sinister grin and smile on his face.

"Now that's gangsta shit to the fullest! You must have heard stories about me!" Vontez said and they shared a laugh again.

"Speaking of ladies *Bruh*, I know your squad still playing their roles, ain't they?" Verdale asked his brother.

"You already know Lil *Bruh*! Stephanie and Keisha are running the operations of Urban Styles. They just sent me a print-out of last quarter's earnings. Business is doing rather well, I must say. You know black women love their weave!" Vontez joked and continued, "Remaining friends with those two was the best thing I could've done. They really have been beneficial to a brotha!"

Vontez had brief relationships with both women, at separate times of course. In both women, he found similarities. Both women were beautiful, ambitious hair stylists with a flair for fashion and both were business minded. Although they hadn't worked out as a couple, Vontez saw them as perfect fits for his Beauty and Barber and Hair Store venture. Putting their personal differences aside, the three formed a formidable trio. Sharing a love of shopping, high fashion and healthy profits, the two women quickly became more than business associates. A friendship of kindred spirits, coupled with a mutual love and respect for Vontez produced a relationship of sisterhood between the divas. This relationship was marveled at by insiders, who were privy to the whole story of the three willing parties.

What started off strictly as a business venture, morphed into Big Love. Vontez's issue of infidelity because of his more than healthy sexual appetite, in both relationships with Keisha and Stephanie wouldn't be an issue anymore, with both women fulfilling his every sexual desire as well as their own lustful fantasies. They stumbled across this realization after going out for cocktails after a business meeting, during the infancy stages of Urban Styles. The three went to "Joe's Crab Shack" after locking in a wholesale hair supplier out of Chicago. After a couple of Category 5's, the preferred drink of choice of the trio, the flirting of the ladies toward Vontez was vividly apparent. It was as if an unspoken challenge had been waged by the two women and Vontez was their conquest.

After leaving Joe's, the three caught a cab back to their hotel in downtown Chicago. Vontez, who was keenly aware of what was about to transpire, played his role to a tee...asking the ladies back to his suite, to smoke some Sour Diesel he had brought along for the trip. The ladies obliged, without hesitation.

Before the blunt was halfway smoked Stephanie said, "That hot tub looks big enough for four people."

Keisha right on cue said, "Well three shouldn't be any problem then!"

She starts to run the water and goes to the bathroom in search of bubble bath. Vontez, sensing that things were coming to a head, calls for room service ordering two bottles of champagne on ice and an extra-large fruit tray with extra whip cream. Keisha returns from the bathroom with bubble bath in hand, to find Stephanie massaging Vontez's shoulders as he finishes the phone call to room service. Without saying a word verbally, although turned on by the sight of the brown skin bombshell in black lace panties and bra rubbing on their soon-to-be shared lover, Keisha's eyes spoke volumes. She stared for a couple of seconds, and it felt like hours as she visually critiqued Stephanie's attributes.

Stephanie's skin was caramel brown, with the 18 inch Remy sew-in she was *rockin'*; she looked like Kenya Moore off of 'Atlanta Housewives'. Her size 8 frame was curved in all the right places. Size 34C breasts stood firm in a black lace bra, and she imagined they would remain that way once the bra was removed. The arch in the small of her back seem to have dimples that led to her round plump ass, that was 87 in her jeans. But now, in plain sight, it left her mouth watering as thoughts of licking the round mounds filled her head.

Stephanie must have read Keisha's mind, as the women's eyes met in a gaze of lust. Keisha's light-skin complexion and flawless skin had had Stephanie in awe all night during dinner. But now as their eyes met and Keisha peeled off her black and red dress while staring at them both, revealing a frame equal to that of "Maliah", Stephanie's pussy started moistening instantly. And although being with a woman had not been in her plans, she was geeked with anticipation.

Keisha, slightly shorter than Stephanie's 5'7", stood at 5'5", size 11-12, with size 38D voluptuous breast with pinkish brown nipples the size of nickels. Her stomach was flat and that only accentuated the shape of her hips, fat ass and thick thighs. After revealing herself, to Vontez and Stephanie's delight, Keisha poured some bubble-bath in the slow running hot-tub and said, "Oh, so y'all *gonna* start without me?" She picked up the ashed half-smoked blunt, lit it and sashayed her way to the edge of the side of the bed, sitting beside Stephanie and Vontez.

"Let me give you a shotgun," Keisha seductively asked Stephanie, as she deeply inhaled the Sour Diesel stick.

As their lips touched, Stephanie inhaled the thick smoke from Keisha's mouth. Keisha's tongue followed the smoke and entered Stephanie's mouth, only to be met by Stephanie's own taster. The two women kissed passionately, losing themselves in their five senses, as they touched each other with gentleness, a feeling only another woman's touch could create. They tasted the sweet liquor and Sour Diesel marijuana from each other's lips and mouths. Their sweet smelling body lotions and perfumes were intoxicating. The sounds of their mutual moans had both ladies crevices soaking wet, as well as Vontez's manhood standing at full attention. Their eyes met, as they separated from the sensual kiss, and both knew that they had just reached a level of intimacy that they were both longing for. At that moment they knew that the bond that had just been formed was indeed unbreakable.

A knock on the door brought the women out of their lustful daze and Vontez gets up and asks, "Who is it?" "Room service!" a sultry voice replies.

Vontez looks out the peephole to confirm and cracks the door open. He hands the extremely attractive Puerto Rican lady a $20 bill as a tip and says, "Just leave the cart Sweetheart!"

She looks at the denomination of the bill in her hand and says, "No problem Sir!" and turns to walk away, only for Vontez to notice her "J-Lo-ish" figure. She walks down the hall toward the elevator. Vontez couldn't help but smile because if he didn't have two bad bitches on the other side of the door, he would have knocked shorty.

Vontez turned around to see Keisha's face buried in Stephanie's cleanly shaven pussy. Stephanie's legs were spread full-eagle, while Keisha was face down, ass up in a doggy style pose. The sounds of ecstasy were filling the room and Vontez's dick stiffened. He moved closer to the ladies, dropping the remainder of his clothes to the floor with each step until he stood completely naked directly behind Keisha's tooted ass. He gently removed her soaked red thong, with her lifting one knee at a time, giving him the assistance he needed, so he wouldn't clumsily interrupt their activities.

The love juices were oozing from Keisha's crevice and Vontez entered her moist, warm pussy and Keisha let out a pleasing moan. Filling her entirely, Vontez could feel Keisha's pussy walls pulsating with pleasure, as he stroked in and out of her. The deeper he stroked, the faster she flickered her tongue across Stephanie's clitoris, causing an erotic symphony of sounds that the hotel walls couldn't hold.

As Vontez straddled Keisha from behind, Stephanie looked into his eyes and mouthed the words, "I'm *bout* to cum Papi!" As Stephanie came, the juices squirted in Keisha's face and she went into a lustful frenzy....sucking and swallowing all of the juices she could devour.

Vontez could feel Keisha's pussy walls tightening, as they did when she would climax. And climax she did! Letting out a long seductive moan as she came. The force of her *cummin'* was forcing Vontez's dick out of her, and her juices found escape routes around his bell-head, causing him to dig deeper, until he finally exploded inside her. As they all collapsed, after an extremely fulfilling lovemaking session, Vontez broke the monotony of heavy breathing and panting by saying, "now, that's what I call a chain reaction!" The girls giggled, as they tried to catch their breaths. They made love to each other for hours, playing an X-rated game of Twister of sorts.

The night vanished and as the sun was rising, the evening of grandeur was culminated with both ladies orally pleasuring Vontez. Each lady licking, sucking and salivating on Vontez's Candy stick. With Keisha licking his balls and Stephanie taking Vontez's manhood in and out of her mouth, to the back of her throat, Vontez's volcano erupted. Seeing the thick cum dripping from Stephanie's lips, Keisha took over and sucked the stream of *cum* out of him, until Vontez was left twitching from the glorious display of affection. That night the three fell in love with each other. Each for various reasons, but all with a unified commitment.

Vontez smiled from ear to ear, as thoughts of his two ladies clouded his train of thought, "yeah, *Bruh*, they'll be here next week to see me."

Verdale, himself quite the lady's man in college, was always impressed by his brother's charisma. A charismatic force that had left two beautiful, intelligent divas at his big brother's disposal.

Vontez forced himself out of his thoughts to ask the question, "How's business?"

Since Snake had turned on them, they had to change up the operation, not knowing what information he had given to authorities. What used to be shipments via UPS to the various hair stores, had now become semi-trucks delivering shipments to warehouses.

"Business is real good right now *Bruh*. We just finalized a warehouse in Lima, so with the one in Hebron and Nap-town that will make three hubs," Verdale said with a 'money-making' grin on his face.

The brothers operation was not limited to one city or state. Their reach was more of a regional nature. They had team members as far north as Detroit, as far south as

Atlanta, as far west as Chicago and as far east as Charlotte. Their operation was moving upwards of 250 kilos a month, with the plethora of outlets. The beauty of it all was that the out-of-town players in their game would come pick up the product from one of the hubs. They usually sent reliable, trustworthy drivers with the money and the product would be placed inside of the compartment filled stash-cars. Each hub was equipped with well trained workers, that were compensated handsomely, for their efficient efforts; thus cutting the act of betrayal to virtually none.

Vontez had set some gruesome examples of men foolish enough to violate his code of trust. That's why they had to be meticulous in the planning of the inevitable execution of Snake, so the trail of suspicion wouldn't lead back to them.

"That's what's up, *Bruh*. One monkey don't stop no show! I don't know what the fuck Snake's ass was thinking, or maybe he wasn't. The nigga had to be using his own product or something, *'cause* any *muthafucka* in their right mind knows not to fuck wit the family!" Vontez said with conviction in his voice.

"You probably right *Bruh*, but we *gonna* get to the bottom of this shit! And his ass *gonna* be *sittin'* at the bottom of the Ohio River soon, real soon!" replied Verdale with his facial expression emphasizing that he meant what he said.

"What's good with Flash? Tell him I said what's up!" Vontez said.

"I will. He's good though. Him, his wife, and the kids just came back from Costa Rica on one of those Disney Cruise Ships. He said they had a ball! Me, Gina and the kids are going with them on the next one in May. I'm already *lookin'* forward to it," exclaimed Verdale.

"Be sure to take some pics for me *Bruh*, I love that ocean scenery. Me and the girls had a blast when we took the Jamaican Cruise, even though we barely left the room the first couple of days", Vontez said with a little snicker.

"You know I got you," Verdale said to his brother.

For the next couple of hours, until the visit was over, the brothers small-talked about everything from business expansion to who was there from their city in the prison camp, to how the Bengals were going to fair this football season, and everything in between. They gave each other a brotherly embrace and said goodbye as they ended their monthly ritual.

Vontez departed behind the prisoner's exit door. Verdale left the visiting room happy to see his brother in good shape mentally, physically and spiritually. Both men had strong faith, having been brought up in the church. They believed that everything happened for a reason especially when things were totally out of their control.

As Verdale hopped back in his SUV, he surveyed the landscape of the penitentiary and its surroundings. He thought to himself, this place is an oxymoron. How could such a beautiful place house the ugliness of a prison?

Chapter 2

"Man that was a bad lil bitch you left the spot wit last night. I know you tapped that?" Tiny asked Luke, as if he already knew the answer.

Luke and Tiny were bouncers at Snake's club called the "Snake Pit". Luke was notorious for his story telling of his sexual exploits with patrons from the club, something that was a normal occurrence for the club's security team.

It was an early Saturday afternoon and Precious, the bartender, was busy stocking the bar and enjoying the tall tales of Luke. She was a cute, petite light brown-skin girl, with hazel eyes that reminded everyone of a young Jada Pinkett. Luke and Tiny were offensive lineman sized dudes. Tiny wore braids and Luke wore a low Caesar cut. Both were brown-skinned, Luke being slightly darker than Tiny. The guys doubled as security and cleaning staff, and that's what they were in the process of doing this Saturday morning. With brooms in hand, the men continued their conversation.

Luke as animated as ever started in with, "shorty was bad as fuck and she was live! Man you know I don't take hoes back to the spot and I didn't want to come out of pocket for a room so we went back to her spot. I was skep at first, because she stay on the Eastside of Broadway, down by the projects. It was like a block away, so I wasn't trippin'. The whole way over, shorty was feeling me up, *talkin'* bout what she *gonna* do to this dick when we get to her spot. Man I was harder than a muthafucka. So we pull up to the spot, it's a two-family on Pinecrest Avenue. It was a decent lil spot fo'real *doe*! I mean shorty's shit was laid out, black leather pit, 60" flat screen on the wall, a marble dining room table, and the bathroom and kitchen was clean as fuck! She had a California King sized bed with a 5 piece bedroom set, all black with gold trim...I was like damn! I just knew that shorty was *fuckin'* wit a baller!" So she was like, "do you want something to drink?" I was like, "hell yeah, what you got?" She was like, "would you like a Mimosa?" I didn't even know what the fuck a Mimosa was, but I was like, "hell, yeah!"

Precious the bartender couldn't help but snicker.

"Man, so I roll up some of that Black Diamond OG Kush that I had and we listened to some Trey Songz on Pandora, while sitting on the couch. Shorty get to *tellin'* me that she don't usually get down like this, but she been peeped me at the club, but she was in a relationship then. She tells me that she's in school to be a nurse and that she work at University, as a PCA on 2nd shift. *Shid*! I was thinking that shorty sounds like a keeper fo'real *doe*! And the nigga she just broke up wit must have been thinking the same thing, because her phone gets to *blowin'* up.

"Dude called about ten times back to back. Shorty gets to apologizing and shit, saying how they been broke up for a couple of weeks. The nigga used to get drunk and whoop her ass sometimes. She said she deserved better and was through wit his ass.

Next thing I know, this nigga *bangin'* on the door and her phone still ringing. It's her Ex! Man, I was like, "here we go with this shit!" Luckily I keep my *Nina* on me. So I was ready for whatever. She answers her phone and let that Nigga have it! That one way! *Talkin'* bout, "if you don't get your little dick ass away from my house! Wit *yo' stalkin'* ass! You didn't appreciate me when you had me, so make like Michael Jackson and beat it Nigga!"

Man I was weak-as-fuck, when she said that shit. Anyway dude begged for a hot-minute, then I guess his pride must have kicked in, 'cause he was like, "Fuck you, you *stankin'* pussy ass bitch!" then he bounced.

After all that drama I wasn't even feeling it fo'real. Shorty mush have read the look on my face, 'cause she got to *sayin'* how sorry she was and that she was really feeling me and how she hoped that this wouldn't mess things up between us. Man before I could even say a word, shorty was *unzippin'* my pants and pulling my dick out! She sucked the fuck out this dick! On some super head type shit!

Shid, when I said I was about to bust, she went hard in the paint! She swallowed all that shit and kept going until I got hard again. She must have slipped her panties off while she was giving me head, unless she didn't have any on in the first place. But she took the dick out her mouth and stood up, while stroking this *muthafucka* and straddled me like a *fuckin'* racehorse jockey! Man, she rode me like she was going for the *muthafuckin* "Triple Crown" Homie!" Luke, Tiny and Precious all laughed in unison.

"Damn you a dirty-dick ass Nigga! *'Cause* I know you didn't wear no rubber, with *yo'* trifling ass!" Precious playfully scolded.

"She didn't look like she had shit!" Luke said with hood ignorance in his voice.

In the midst of the three club employees joking with each other, in walks Snake. Precious was the first one to notice his entrance and said, "Hey Snake! How you *doin'* today?"

"I'm good Lil Mama! How about you", he replies.

"I'm good too, just trying to stock up this bar. It was a full house in here last night. I think those new radio spots are working!" Precious said with exuberance.

"Yeah, I think you're right Lil Mama, things have been *jumpin'* lately," Snake answered her.

"What's up fellas," Snake acknowledged his two security workers.

"What up Boss?"

"What's good Snake?" the men respectfully replied as Snake disappeared into his back office.

Snake relocated to Louisville shortly after Vontez was convicted. He had family in Louisville and a few power licks in the city. Although only 100 or so miles away, Louisville was about five or six years behind Cincinnati, in fashion trends, club scenes and everyday way of life.

Louisville still had gang bangers and that was so 1980-ish. Snake was given immunity from any prosecution by the RENU agency, under the stipulation he would work for them from time-to-time. They would keep him supplied with the product as long as he gave them a big-fish at least once a year, which he had no problem doing.

Louisville was the perfect city for him to set-up in because it was wide-open, plus he already had connections there and it was right on the edge of RENU's jurisdiction.

Snake's selfishness and greed were key attributes to fuel his plans to tell on rival major players and steal their clientele. Once his competitors got too big, it was inevitable that they would come tumbling down. Snake's cousin Jerome was his link to the Louisville drug circle. Jerome used to middle-man Brick Deals thru Snake and make himself a few thousand off of each deal. When Snake told him he was thinking about relocating to the city for a fresh start, Jerome urged him to do so, with lofty notions of his own success through association. Unaware that his cousin was now a Star Playa for the other team...the police!

The small club that Snake leased was Jerome's brainchild. Jerome saw it as a perfect camouflage to launder money. Snake saw it as a way to keep an eye on who was getting money in the town. Jerome and Snake ran the club together. Jerome was in charge of ordering the liquor and hiring staff. While Snake handled the promotions, advertisement and the majority of the money. Jerome had been the one to hire Candy, the newest barmaid, and Sapphire, the newest dancer. Both were conspirators in Verdale's plan of revenge for his brother.

Snake, a well-groomed brotha in his early 40's, with brown skin, of average height and build, was quite the ladies' man and reminded you of the crooner, Keith Washington. Being a top-notch brotha himself, he only went for intelligent, beautiful and immaculately groomed women. Hoodrats couldn't even give him head. So when Jerome hired Candy and Sapphire, Snake was impressed. They stood out to him, in a good way. Candy was light-skin, with a slim build, but she had some hips and ass.

Her complexion, full-lips and naturally curly hair reminded him of the singer "Mya". Sapphire was a thick chocolate bombshell that exuded "sex appeal". When he first saw her he could have sworn she was "Black Chyna", who had appeared in <u>Black Men Magazine</u>.

Both women were college students at the University of Louisville. They brought a level of stature to the club because they weren't your average ran thru *hoodrats*. Snake had already set his sights on the two girls with Candy being more of his type because she kept her clothes on, although he had to admit to himself that Sapphire could get it. Snake, lost in his thoughts, was brought back to reality upon hearing Jerome's voice as he entered the open door of the office.

"What's up Cuz?" Jerome said as he closed the door behind him.

As Jerome sits a black briefcase on the desk he says, "Here's sixty thousand for two of 'em. I still owe down for three. I'll be done by the middle of the week, at the latest by Friday."

"That's what it do Fam. I see *ya handlin'* things," Snake said proudly of his cousin's performance in the game.

"I heard them West-side Niggas was beefin', what's up with that shit," continued Snake.

"Don't worry I squashed that! I had a sit-down with a couple of head-honchos on the Westside, and they said that two of their little Niggas got into it over some chick. They said that shit was put to rest. Not now but right now! They realize that that shit ain't good for business, with gun play involved the *"Boys"* will be *hangin'* in the hood too close," Jerome said in a street savvy tone

"Ok den, what was it some Blood and Crip shit or something?" curiously asked Snake.

"Naw, both them Niggas is "True Blue" Westside Niggas, most of the Bloods run on the Eastside," answered Jerome.

"Alright Cuz, you know we don't get down like that in my city. It might be some small neighborhood squabbles like Avondale vs Madisonville or The Fay vs English Woods but the only color we fighting for is that green dolla on da real!" Snake told his cousin.

"I heard that!" Jerome says emphatically.

"*Cause* in the end that's the only color that counts," Snake added for emphasis. Snake continued by saying, "I've been meaning to ask you about the two new girls, which one you done snatched up?"

Jerome chuckled before answering, "Damn, you already know me cuz. I been trying to crack Sapphire, she's a good girl on some real shit, unless she's just playing hard to get with my ass!"

"What's up with Candy? She seeing anybody," Snake inquired.

"Since when does that matter?" Jerome retorted and they shared a laugh.

"Yeah, you right cuz. I just wasn't trying to step on any toes, that's all," Snake said condescendingly.

"So how do you think things are *gonna* turn out for the Halloween Bash? I've been hearing the radio spots *runnin'* heavy in the rotation," Jerome asked as he changed the subject.

"I'm pretty confident that it's *gonna* be live. We need to get extra security in here for that shit *doe*. Niggas in my city always take advantage of being able to walk around freely with a *muthafuckin'* mask on to be on some bullshit! I know "The Ville" ain't no different, so we gotta be on point Fam you feel me," stated Snake.

"That's what's up! I'll make sure we double the security that night," Jerome replied.

Meanwhile........

"Girl, I see that nigga Jerome at *yo'* ass strong, don't fuck around and catch real feelings for that Nigga. Bitch you hear me? We on a *muthafuckin'* mission! That's it, that's all," Candy said emphatically.

"Bitch, I hear you! Ain't *nothin'* wrong with getting a couple of gifts here and there and getting wined and dined, shit! I just look at it as "job perks" for a Bitch! As a matter of fact when you *gonna* make *yo'* move on that lame-ass Snake, with his fine pretty-boy ass," Sapphire questioned.

"*Dat* Nigga is fine Girl, wit his *snitchin'* ass! Don't worry I ain't *gonna* be one of them thirsty hoes. Anyway the plan was for him to choose one of us, but you got his cousin nose wide da fuck open now, so I guess it's on me."

Candy continued, "And after he see this naughty school-girl outfit at the Halloween party, he'll be checking for a Bitch! Plus you know he don't fuck wit *hoodrats*, so I got to play my position to a tee, to make that nigga yearn for this pussy!"

"I know that's right!" replied Sapphire and the girls giggled together.

"You heard from E-Tone last night?" Sapphire inquired.

"They'll be down here this week to drop some money off for these bills, plus I told *'em* about the Halloween party. They probably *gonna* make a cameo just to peep the layout in person. You know how them niggas work," declared Candy.

Verdale's hitmen, E-Tone and J.J. had set the girls up in a two bedroom condo about twenty minutes from campus, just to make shit look official, with Verdale funding the whole operation, of course. He would spare no expense to avenge his brother's betrayal.

"What's your schedule look like this week Candy," Sapphire asked.

"They got me on the schedule for $2 Tuesdays and $3 Thursdays so far and I'm on standby for Saturdays, starting next week. What about you," asked Candy?

"Just Mondays and Wednesdays, since those the only nights they have dancers," replied Sapphire.

"Well do you want to ride back to the "Nati" tonight to party or what? I know them Niggas missing us up there," Candy announced.

"I know they is, but I got plans with Jerome later. I'm going to meet him at the club tonight around 9pm, then we're supposed to go to dinner, then come back to the club for some drinks," replied Sapphire.

"Ok den Bitch, don't fall in-love wit that Nigga or the dick! You hear me?" Candy said in a big sister kinda tone.

"Girl, I heard you the first time! Do you want to hit the mall with me before you hit the road or what," asked Sapphire.

"Might as well since we got some extra dough to blow, you feel me?" Candy responded and the girls shared another laugh.

They had been enlisted for the plot by Verdale's "Goon Squad", E-Tone and J.J. because of their beauty and ruthlessness in carrying out diabolical plots. The girls received $1,000 a week for the "Mission", a fully furnished condo and an inconspicuous slider (a piece), plus whatever they made from the club they could keep, not to mention, whatever gifts their unsuspecting victims gave them. All they had to do was set things up for Snake's untimely demise. The girls would've gladly carried out the devious plan of cutting Snake's throat themselves but Verdale wanted his hitmen to put the finishing touches on a dish best served cold – "revenge"!

The girls were being used as a smoke-screen, so that the crime couldn't be connected back to the brothers. The Goons could seize the window of opportunity for the best time to strike with vengeance and gain something financially rewarding for both of them. Their motto was "a dead nigga don't need no money", so they would always plot for a "big score" before they ultimately finished off their stigmatized victim.

Snake would be no different and as a matter of fact the Goons would rather enjoy this one, because Snake had been on their side at one point before he made the fatal mistake of biting the hand that fed him.

Chapter 3

"You think this nigga *gonna* show up or what?" asked J.J.

"Oh, he'll show up alright, they always do. It's something about getting new pussy that makes a nigga forget all the rules to the game," E-Tone stated with obvious confidence, as they waited for their next victim to pull up to the recently vacated house located in a cul-de-sac of a sparsely populated residential neighborhood in Lexington.

Latoya had just got off the phone with "Maintain". He was a heavy-hitter in the city who had owed-down for way too long. E-Tone and J.J. had been casing Maintain for more than a month, so they knew where his stash-spot was and other pertinent details. They also knew that he had a high-tech security system, so in order for them to gain access to the mini-fortress Maintain would have to accompany them. They knew Latoya would be his type, being a high-yellow Paula Patton clone, something that any man with bravado would find irresistible. Strategically, Latoya bumped into Maintain at one of his routine Monday mall visits.

*** (**Side note**) When you're in the game, don't become a creature of habit, routine where-a-abouts make you easy pickings for Jack-Boyz. ***

After their initial meeting, all it took were a few extremely graphic, overly forward flirtatious text messages to have Maintain more than ready for their rendezvous.

"He's pulling up now, it's the Black Chrysler 300 coming to the driveway!" yelled Latoya to her accomplices.

"Y'all know the plan, let's get it!" commands E-Tone and they all scurry to their planned positions.

The doorbell rings. Latoya yells, "Its open!"

Maintain opened the door to find an unfurnished house with only a few boxes sitting around in the two rooms before him.

"Excuse my house, I'm in the process of moving in," shouts Latoya from the kitchen. Maintain instantly senses something's not right, like he's been set-up by "Dateline NBC". But the anticipation of getting a chance to knock-off the badass redbone he'd knocked at the mall, made his suspicions disappear. Latoya continues, "Lock the door behind you and come back to the kitchen. I'm putting away my dishes."

With pussy tunnel vision, Maintain blindly walks into the trap. As soon as he enters the kitchen he sees E-Tone's face with a sinister smirk and tries to run back towards the front door. J.J. was already standing at the front entrance with a sawed-off shot gun in hand.

"What the fuck is this? Y'all know who y'all *fuckin'* wit?" Maintain blurts out.

"Yeah, we know who we *fuckin'* wit, Jermaine Thomas! A nigga that think he slicker than oil. A Nigga that think his shit is sweet out this bitch. A Nigga that forgot to pay for them 10 bricks he got fronted! Yeah, we know who we *fuckin'* wit!" E-Tone boldly stated.

"Man, I was *gonna* pay. I swear I was. I tried to call Dale but his number was in my other phone that I lost. Man I swear on everything!"

"Nigga that was over four months ago, and my folks been *tryin'* to call *yo'* ass! Why didn't you get the same number on your new phone Homeboy?" E-Tone said with sarcasm.

"I, I, I uumh!" stuttered Maintain as if his mind couldn't think of a lie fast enough.

"I, I, I, what?" mocked E-Tone. "I tell you what, since I'm a nice guy and all, *I'ma* give you a break. You take us down to *yo'* stash spot at the self-storage on Lincoln Road and I won't kill your son, Jermaine Jr. that goes to Hayes Elementary and gets out of school at 2:45. I won't pay *yo'* Mama, Ms. Lisa, a visit when she gets off at 4:30p.m. from the paper factory on 12th street. We'll see how well you cooperate before we decide *yo'* fate. How about it my G? The choice is yours," E-Tone said coldly.

"Man, please don't hurt my son and my Mama. I'll give y'all everything I swear!" begged Maintain.

"Oh, now you wanna pay up! Ok, cool. Let's go!" E-Tone commanded.

They piled in Maintain's Chrysler 300 but not before J.J. searched the vehicle finding the 40 cal Maintain had tucked under the front seat. Latoya drove, E-Tone sat next to her in the front seat and Maintain and J.J. sat in the rear. It was the longest 15 minutes in Maintain's life and unfortunately they would be his last. Once they reached the unmonitored self-storage, Maintain entered the electronic combination and the door was lifted automatically. Upon inspection, behind what looked like two apartments full of furniture sat two floor safes under a comforter.

"Unlock them bitches and don't forget *yo'* Mama and son's lives depend on this shit, so don't get brave now Nigga!" barked E-Tone.

Maintain entered both combinations and stepped back from the safes with J.J.'s shotgun still at his back. E-Tone opened the first door and saw stacks of money and calmly said, "Jack Pot." He opened the 2nd safe and saw bricks still unopened and a few loose ounces. He looked at Maintain and said, "I'm a man of my word, so *I'ma* put *yo'* mind at ease. *Yo'* Mama and son will not be harmed, I can promise you that. But you on the other hand ain't *gonna* be so lucky. But, I'll tell you what, since you cooperated *I'ma* give you a choice. You can take some of these bullets and have a closed casket funeral or you can snort one of those ounces of powder and go out feeling good and looking good. The choice is yours my G!" declared E-Tone.

As if already knowing what decision he would make, E-Tone grabs an office chair out of the pile of furniture and removed an ounce from the safe, tossing it to Maintain.

"Have a seat homeboy and enjoy yourself one last time *'cause* it's time to pay the piper," E-Tone said with conviction.

Maintain sat down in the chair and began to pray before he buried his face in the 90% pure cocaine. After he lifted his head, the effects were kicking in. He thought about putting up a fight but he knew the results were inevitable and he wanted his family to be able to pay respects to his fully intact corpse. He thought about his greedy, selfish minded decisions that led him to his dreadful fate. Before he inhaled the crystalized powdery substance for the last time, he thought about how he had been the 'cause of his own demise. The second and last time he raised his head, his eyes rolled back and his body began to shake violently in convulsions that lasted for about thirty seconds and it was over.

E-Tone commanded Latoya to empty a gym bag that he spotted in the corner of the storage unit and they filled it with the contents of the safes. E-Tone, having somewhat of a heart, ironically left the storage unit door half open so that the body would be discovered in a timely manner, so that Maintain could have the open casket funeral that he had earned.

Chapter 4

As Valencia pulled up to Mt. Calvary Baptist church at 10:40 a.m. Sunday morning, the sun was shining and the birds were chirping noisily on an unusually warm fall day. Valencia swore she could feel the Holy Spirit from the church parking lot. After parking her silver 2013 Cadillac SRX, she looked in the rearview mirror to adjust her hat and double check her make-up. Feeling content with her appearance, Valencia exited the vehicle and made her way to the church door.

The closer she got to the door, the louder she could hear the music and one of her favorite church hymns was playing, "Order My Steps In Your Word".

"How are you this morning Ms. Valencia?"

"I'm blessed and highly favored," she responded in her best church-lady voice.

She made her way to the sanctuary and sat three pews from the front, and to her astonishment she spotted Verdale, Regina and the twins. They exchanged smiles and she hurried to join them with growing pride in each step.

She asked, "Why didn't you tell me y'all was coming?"

"I wanted it to be a surprise Mama. Surprise!" Verdale answered her jokingly.

"How you doing Mama V?" asked Gina.

"Just fine honey. I see you done lost all that baby weight girl! What you been doing? Zumba or something?" Valencia asked wittingly.

"Mama V you still crazy! Naw, Dale got me a treadmill for the house and I just been watching what I eat, but thanks for noticing," Gina replied.

"Ahh, look at my babies! They look like y'all both done spit 'em out! Chris look just like Verdale when he as a baby and that girl Chrissy look like a mini you Gina, and they getting so big to be just 6 months. What y'all feeding 'em over there some Bill Jack?" a wise cracking Valencia asked.

"Mama, you silly!" Verdale said in a whisper as to not disturb the rest of the congregation.

Valencia grabbed Chris and sat in between Verdale and Gina and they all turned their attention to the Reverend as he stood up from his sitting position on the podium.

Pastor Williams begins his sermon, "Good morning God's people!"

The congregation responds with, "Good Morning pastor!"

The pastor continues, "I had written a sermon last night about another topic, but when I rose from my slumber God put something different on my heart. Many times when we greet people in passing or in other settings, that greeting can set the tone for the encounter. Simply because your words have power. Can I get an Amen this morning?" and the congregation responds with a barrage of Amens.

"As small children we are taught that words are a form of communication and although that might be true to a certain extent, words have power! We've all heard the story of the little train that could. It was a small train that tried to make it up the steep hill, but no matter what, every time the train tried he couldn't muster up enough strength to get up that wretched hill.

Well, as the story goes, the little train had a pep talk with an older train about his dilemma. He shared his issue of not being able to make it up the steep hill and the older train gave him some powerful words of encouragement. He told the little train that in order to make it up that hill he had to first believe that he could do it.

You see some of us count ourselves out of the race before we even hear the starter's gun. Some of us get so down about situations, our finances, our relationships or our job conditions that we give up instead of looking for a solution. But I'm here to tell you today that words have power! Speak life into yourself or friend through words of encouragement. As the story continues the older train told the little train that the next time you come to that hill move forward full steam ahead. And tell yourself you can do it!

Well the little train was apprehensive, but said that he would give it a try. The next day the little train wanted to test this theory so he hit the train tracks heading in the direction of the hill that he so badly wanted to conquer. When he came to the hill he remembered what the older train had told him, to believe in himself. Nervousness kicked in on the little train so he began to talk to himself. He got to saying, "I think I can." As he approached the base of that hill, he gave himself a pep talk because words have power. While the little train kept talking to himself saying, "I think I can" he realized that he was further up that hill than he had ever been before. He gained confidence and said to himself, "I know I can" until he reached the hill's peak.

As humans, as children of God, we have to take on the personality of that little train when we encounter adversity or obstacles. In our life, whatever the situation, you have to believe that you can overcome! You might get weary and give out but whatever you do don't give up! If you got to give yourself a pep talk just to pep yourself up, then do what needs to be done and get back into the race of life and persevere! The Bible says in Proverbs 18 verse 21, "*the tongue has the power of life and death and those who love it will eat its fruit.*" I say words have power, can I get an Amen!"

The congregation responds with a resounding Amen!

Pastor Williams continues, "There's power in your words. Speak life into someone instead of tearing them down with criticism. Just a simple "have a blessed day" or paying someone a compliment, can be enough to give somebody what they need to hear. You don't know what another man or woman is going through in their life but a simple word of positivity can go a long way for someone who was on the verge of suicide. I said words have power! A mother who's frustrated with raising her children on her own appreciates a complement like "you're doing a fine job raising those respectful young men"; those words might be what she needs to hear in order to feel that her efforts are not in vain. Words have Power!"

"When a young brother who might have had a troubled past gets upset at the continuous rejection that he might face trying to find employment and contemplates turning back to the street -- just a simple "young brother, hang in there, don't give up, somethings going to shake for you real soon; just be patient!" That might be enough to keep them from turning back to a life of crime. Words have Power! The Bible says in Proverbs 12 verse 18, *"the words of the reckless pierce like swords, but the tongue of the wise brings healing."* Can I get an Amen?"

After the pastor preached on for about another 25 to 30 minutes, the congregation dispersed, but not before they stood to their feet in exuberation from his well-received message.

While walking from the church to the parking lot, Valencia commented to her son and daughter-in-law "the pastor sho' nuff was preaching today wasn't he?"

Verdale and Gina responded in unison, "yes he was!"

Verdale added, "Mama why don't you ride back to your house with Gina and the kids. I'll take your car and go pick up the chicken and meet you guys back at the house. How's that sound to you?"

"Sounds like a plan to me son. Don't be out joy riding in my whip, *ya* dig?" Valencia playfully responded.

"I'll see y'all in a minute," Verdale retorted with a chuckle.

Chapter 5

Sapphire and Jerome had been dating for a couple weeks now and she was getting to see a side of him she never imagined he would possess. Jerome was a warm, passionate, goal oriented romantic and determined man that had come from very humble beginnings. The similarities they shared were many and she thought about what life would be like under different circumstances. She thought about how they could live happily ever after, if it wasn't for that one small hiccup; she was there to rock his cousin to sleep, a permanent sleep!

It was a Saturday night and both Sapphire and Candy were getting dressed for the evening. Sapphire was going out with Jerome again and Candy was getting ready to go to work at the club.

"Girl, that's a bad-ass dress right there! Where y'all going tonight?" asked Candy.

"Jerome's taking me to dinner at this exclusive Italian restaurant along the river. Then from there we're going to see Jill Scott perform at the Palace Theater," Candy answered with all smiles.

Her dress was a black and silver sequined gown; off the shoulder and formfitting. She was filling it out to perfection. Jerome and her had went shopping earlier in the week for her outfit and accessories, which included a white gold necklace with a diamond teardrop pendant and matching earrings. He also purchased Sapphire the Mark Jacob purse and matching stilettos, both black. She was the epitome of Nubian elegance and it made her feel like a princess for the first time since she played dress up as a little girl.

Sapphire was from a very modest lower middle-class neighborhood called Fairmount, located on the west side of Cincinnati. She had never been exposed to anything more than the bare necessities before meeting Candy when they were 16 and both working at McDonald's. Candy grew up under similar circumstances. She grew up in the Over-the-Rhine area of Cincinnati. This area was a poverty filled neighborhood full of working class people who were overworked and under paid. When Sapphire initially met Candy, she wondered how a girl could afford new Jordan's every time they came out off a part-time Mickey D's job. She figured that she must have a dope boy boyfriend or something.

One night when the girls were cleaning up after closing she asked Candy how she stays so fly. Candy, reluctant at first, shared the source of her extra earnings with her friend. She told her that her cousin Tino and his crew were Jack Boyz, and she would assist them when needed. She explained to Sapphire that her role was simple. They would show her who to befriend and she would usually text her cousin when her and their chosen victim were out on a date, leaving his house vulnerable for a break in. Or, if they didn't know where their victim laid his head, she would get the address for them and they would take care of the rest. At any rate she was always compensated for her part.

Candy told Sapphire that because of her grown-woman's body she would make good bait and that she would ask her cousin to give her a shot. Once Sapphire pulled her first set-up job she was hooked. Incidentally, Candy's cousin Tino was killed in a botched robbery attempt a couple of years later. Already addicted to the money, Candy and Sapphire stayed in cahoots with her cousin's crew members, E-Tone and J.J.

"Girl help me with this up do," Sapphire asked of Candy.

"Bitch, I have to admit you look good fo'real and the up do is going to set off that dress. I got you!" replied Candy, as she helped Sapphire with her hair. Upon completion, they both looked in the mirror with Sapphire still seated and Candy standing behind her like a proud sister.

"Candy, look at me. I look like a sophisticated debutante!" an exuberant Sapphire stated.

"Yes, you do! Beautiful," replied Candy.

Sapphire stood to further admire herself in the full-length mirror. She told herself that she deserved this type of life and not just in bits and pieces. Her phone rings and she sees Jerome's face pop up on her screen.

"I'll be right down," she says to a smitten Jerome on the other end.

"You have a nice time tonight girl and don't forget we on a mission ok!" Candy said, even though she could tell her best friend was already on the brink of being head-over-heels for their target's cousin.

When Sapphire got downstairs, the doorman's eyes were bulging out of his head when she stepped out of the elevator.

"You look stunning Ms. Turner, simply stunning," remarked Elliot the doorman, as he followed her to the front door and opened it. Jerome exited his cocaine white 5500 Mercedes Benz with a white box in hand and met Sapphire at the front door.

"Damn, Babe you look gorgeous! I have another surprise for you!" Jerome said with excitement, and they stepped back inside the building to escape the chill of the night air. Jerome removed the black shawl that Candy had on to cover her bare shoulders and removed a short black mink coat from the white box.

"Oh my God Jerome! It's beautiful!" Sapphire screams with excitement.

"Nothing but the best for my lady" Jerome said as he placed the mink coat over the shoulders of Sapphire and put the shawl in the box.

They left the building and Jerome opened the door for Sapphire, like the perfect gentleman he intended to be that night. He placed the box in the trunk and got in the driver's seat and their fairytale night began. The debonair Jerome, in his tailor-made Armani suit and the exquisite Sapphire turned heads all night; at first at dinner, where they were treated like celebrities, and then again at the concert where they were treated like royalty. This was due in part to the VIP booth in the balcony that Jerome had sprung for. Sapphire had to admit that he certainly knew how to treat a lady and that's exactly what he made her feel like.

After leaving the concert they waited out front for the valet to bring the car around. Once inside the vehicle Sapphire began the conversation.

"Jerome, I wanna thank you for a wonderful night. I mean I've never felt so special and so regal in my whole life. You've been so sweet and patient these past few weeks, and I just want you to know that as much as I've tried to play tough and nonchalant about it, I can't even begin to see myself with anyone else but you. I guess I'm rambling, but baby I think I love you!"

"I've been waiting to hear those words since the moment I first laid eyes on you. Everyday we're together I want you to feel like the queen you are Sapphire," Jerome said with sincerity.

"Ahh Romey!" And the two embraced in a passionate kiss. "I don't want this night to ever end" Sapphire said seductively.

Jerome replied in his best Denzel voice, "It doesn't have to".

Jerome's mind was racing with thoughts of exploring Sapphire's enticing body. Up until this point a few intense kisses had been the extent of their sexual exploits together, but tonight they had crossed over into a new realm in their relationship and Jerome had every intention of consummating their new endeavor.

After a 20 minute drive filled with impassioned kisses and stirring stares, they pulled into the driveway of Jerome's home and he hit the garage door opener, revealing his Lincoln Navigator and chromed out Harley bike. He pulled in next to his other means of transportation and the garage door closed behind them.

Entering the house through the door attached to the garage led them directly to Jerome's kitchen. Sapphire was impressed with the décor of her new boyfriend's four bedroom home. The art-deco furnishings were breathtaking to her. She was definitely feeling his style.

"Would you like a drink sweetheart?" Jerome asked, breaking into Sapphire's thoughts.

"Let's do some shots baby," Sapphire seductively replied.

"Let me guess -- 1800 Silver?" Jerome said as he smiled.

"You know it?" Sapphire exclaimed and they shared a laugh.

Jerome put on Pandora Radio and after a few shots, he and Sapphire were up slow dancing and kissing in the middle of the living room.

'I'm so happy that you came into my life Romey. You're everything I could've asked for in a man!" Sapphire says with glazed eyes.

"I feel the same way Sapphire; I feel a special connection to you for some reason. I just feel like I can be myself when I'm with you. Like I can let my guard down."

Sapphire stared into Jerome's eyes and tears formed, partly because she knew her initial intentions weren't genuine and partly because now that she had fallen in love with him, she couldn't go through with the plan of killing his cousin or could she?

Jerome softly kissed Sapphire and then turned her around and slowly unzipped the beautiful sequined gown, letting it drop to the floor. Sapphire, shoeless already, stepped out of the perimeter of the gown that lay at her feet. She stepped closer to her man who stood there in a wife-beater and his slacks. She went straight to his belt, unfastening it and removing his pants from him. She lowered his boxer briefs and took his half stiffened penis in her mouth. She took him into the back of her throat, letting her throat muscles massage his head until he was full mast, doubling the length of his impressive manhood.

Jerome looked down in amazement at the remarkable deep-throat skills of Sapphire as she took him in and out of her juicy mouth. He felt himself about to prematurely explode, so he gently pulled Sapphire's suction cup lips off his phallus and lifted her up. He walked over to the couch and placed her down, he flipped her over on her stomach and lifted her hips removing her cum soaked panties. Sapphire's ass was tooted up exposing one of the prettiest pussies that Jerome had ever seen. Her pussy lips were puffy and the landing strip of hair that remained on her manicured love cave looked like strands of moist silk as Jerome examined closer. The sweet aroma that exuded from her love crevice was more intoxicating than the tequila they had just drank.

Jerome's tongue found its mark as Sapphire moaned with pleasure. He licked up and down each crease and crevice of her pussy lips until he finally settled on her clit. Once there her moans of pleasure dramatically increased as did his sensual intensity.

"Damn Romey! Suck that pussy Baby! I'm about to cream for you!" Sapphire managed to say in between gasps of air as she began to ooze her love juices.

Jerome, tasting her cum, stood up and entered her from behind until he hit the bottom of her pussy as she let out a whimper in ecstasy. Jerome couldn't hold back any longer after a couple of minutes of the mind-blowing sex and yelled out, "I'm *cummin'* baby!"

Sapphire, with cat-like reflexes, dismounted Jerome and spun around and took him in her mouth as he came, swallowing every drop and continued to suck until he was hard again. The intense love making continued all-night long with each lover reaching their climax several times until they finally collapsed in each other's arms. A perfect night of compassion and ecstasy culminated one of the best days of both their lives. A boundless, unbreakable bond was forged thru the intensity of their lovemaking.

Chapter 6

"Come out to the hottest club in the city tonight the Snake Pit for the Masquerade Ball of all masquerade balls, located at 4400 26th street. Tickets are $25 in advance, $35 at the door with cash prizes for the best costumes for males and females. The Snake Pit, located at 4400 26th street for an inner-city upscale event. Advanced tickets can be purchased at the Snake Pit, Simon Says Barber Shop and All-Out Car Detail. Come to the Snake Pit for the Masquerade Ball and celebrate your Halloween night in style at the Snake Pit, where style is a must and having a good time is mandatory! This is a grown and sexy event. Age limit is 25 and up!"

Snake smiled as he pulled up to the club while hearing his radio spot blasting over the airwaves. Today he was driving his charcoal gray Range Rover with the factory

Bose system. It was 6:30 in the evening and doors opened up at 8, so he had arrived just a little early to oversee the final preparations for the night's event. He got out of his vehicle dressed in custom made "Count Blackula" outfit, complete with make-up and fangs. As he walked up to the door he admired the red carpet entrance and velvet rope that graced the front of the club.

The photographer was out front snapping pictures of the security staff who were dressed up as their favorite football players. The six security personnel looked like an All-star offensive linemen crew, with Tiny and Luke leading the theatrics as they posed out front for pictures.

"What's *shakin'* fellas" Snake asked as he walked up to the group of bouncers. They all responded with a barrage of "What's up?" Luke had to be the one to comment on Snake's outfit

"I like that outfit Boss man, you look like Eddie Murphy in a Vampire in Brooklyn," he stated in a harmless sarcastic tone and they all laughed a little.

"Hey, I got an idea Mr. Snake. Why don't you pose in the middle and have the security staff surround you in the next series of photos?" said the photographer.

"Cool and I want a few solo shots too," Snake responded.

The group of men then posed for some photos together. Afterwards Snake posed for his solo photo session.

Luke had gotten the entire staff out front, including Precious, Candy, and all of the other female workers. The four servers were dressed up like cheerleaders and they all had pom-poms in hand. Precious was dressed in a cheetah print body suit with whiskers painted on her face. The skin-tight bodysuit hugged her petite frame in all the right places. Candy was dressed up as a naughty school-girl, complete with the ponytails, the white button-down tied in a knot at her stomach and the red plaid skirt that barely covered her perky posterior. Monique the 3rd bartender was a tall slender girl with a model frame. She was dressed as Wonder Woman and her hips and ass was definitely superhero worthy, to say the least.

Snake was impressed by the staff's creativity and comradery but he was taken back by Candy's sex appeal in her outfit. Candy could tell by the way he gazed at her, so she deliberately posed seductively in front of him, during their impromptu photo shoot. After taking pictures the female staff members and snake all made their way inside. The club was festively decorated for the occasion, with orange and black streamers dropping from the ceiling and several other adornments. Even the D.J. was dressed in a Spiderman outfit. The girls continued taking photos on their cell phones and they were busy posting pictures on Facebook, Instagram and various other social media sites.

Snake approached Candy, who was seated at the end of the bar, scrolling on her phone. "You better be careful tonight Ms. Candy. There's a vampire on the loose", Snake flirtatiously joked.

"I think that vampire better be careful before he bites off more than he can chew," Candy fired back in a sultry voice

"Oh yeah...well I got a sweet tooth and some of Ms. Candy might be just what the doctor ordered", was Snake's come back.

"Is that right, well when are you trying to get that prescription filled, Vampire Playa?" Candy replied as the banter continued between the two.

"How about breakfast tonight after the club closes?" asked Snake.

"I think that can be arranged," said Candy as they exchanged teasing looks.

"Have you seen Rome tonight?" Snake asked Candy.

"No, but him and Sapphire should be here shortly. Speak of the devil, look at Ike and Tina, right on cue," Candy said as Jerome and Sapphire walked through the front door.

"Let me get y'all picture girl. Y'all look so cute together" announced Candy with a couple of the other girls chiming in, including Precious the bartender.

"Y'all *sho* do look cute together..... look at those wigs! Eat the cake! Annie Mae, eat the cake!" she playfully said and got a slew of laughs from the club staff.

Candy took a couple of pictures of the stylish couple.

"Here Candy. Take some on my phone too, girl!" Sapphire said.

"Come on y'all, let's get another group picture, now that Rome and Sapphire are here," Snake announced and they all went out front again for more pictures.

Once the pictures were complete, everyone made their way inside, with Snake and Jerome going to the back office to handle some business. When they came back out to the bar area, the first guest were arriving and within the next two hours the club was packed with party goers. Everybody was having a blast. The radio station was doing a live remote from the club and the line outside extended around the corner.

Snake and Candy were exchanging flirty looks all night long as Candy served alcohol to thirsty patrons. Rome and Sapphire were engrossed in each other, while seated in a private booth. A variety of costumes scattered the club. Every kind of costume you could think of from super heroes, witches, sexy cops, French Maids, gladiators, Avatars, you name it and it was there. Nobody even noticed as E-Tone and J.J. slipped inside dressed in a Scream mask and a Jason mask from Friday the 13th. They ordered a couple of Heinekens and made their way to a corner, where they had a full view of the rest of the establishment.

"This *muthafucka jumpin'* tonight. These, lil country bitches ain't even got shit on as chilly as it is outside" remarked E-Tone to J.J.

"I ain't mad at *'em*. Did you see Candy's fine-ass over there bartending? She still a bad *muthafucka*," J.J. replied.

"Yeah, I saw her, let's just hope Snake think the bitch is fine, so we can get on with this *muthafuckin'* mission", said E-Tone.

"I can dig it, Homie look. There go ole boy right there by the pool table in the Dracula get-up", says J.J.

"This nigga think he a playa even in his Halloween costume, look at this hoe ass nigga! I would let this punk *muthafucka* have it tonight, but you know my motto, if it don't make dollaz, it don't make sense", declared E-Tone as he took a sip of his beer.

"Is that shorty over there, all booed up and shit?" asked J.J.

"Who you talkin bout?" asked E-Tone.

"Sapphire!" States J.J.

"Damn that is her. That must be ole boy's cousin that Candy was *tellin'* me about. Look like she in-love or she doing a *helluva* acting job!" E-Tone says inquiringly.

"Hell, yeah. She got me fooled up in this *muthafucka*. They look like a happy couple to me," adds J.J.

"I ain't *trippin'*; she can keep this nigga occupied while Candy put shit down on his people. It might even work out better that way. This way ain't nobody to pull his coattail to what's going down," E-Tone says, as if he's thinking out loud.

After satisfying themselves with their surveillance, E-Tone and J.J. pick up a couple of scantily dressed hoodrats and vamoosed from the scene. The party was a smashing success with no major incidents. Although there were a couple of minor squabbles, a couple of girls fighting over a popular neighborhood baller and a couple of folks who had gotten too tipsy, had to be escorted out of the club, but other than that the night went on without a hitch.

The winners of the costume contest were a guy dressed like the "King of Pop", Michael Jackson and a young woman dressed like Nikki Ménage, complete with a real booty that would have put Nikki to shame. Towards closing time, Snake came up behind Candy, who was standing behind the bar watching the tail end of a dance battle that had ensued.

He whispered in her ear, "Are you still up for tonight or does the naughty school girl have to be in by curfew?"

"I'm not letting you off that easy. Of course I'm still ready. You're not trying to back out on me are you?" Candy said in a shy school girl voice.

"Ms. Candy, I wouldn't fathom doing such a thing. As a matter of fact why don't you do a countdown on your cash register and I'll be in the office waiting on you," Snake said with a sly tone in his voice.

"Okay, give me about 15 minutes", Candy responded.

After her cash register was counted down, Candy said her goodbyes to the other bartenders and the servers and proceeded to the back office, where Snake was removing the make-up off his face from his Halloween costume.

"You could have kept those fangs in, I wanted to see how they felt when you bite my neck", Candy said in a solicitous tone.

"Oh, yea. That's how you feel? I might just take 'em with us," replies Snake.

After Snake changes clothes, putting on some True Religion jeans, Polo sweater and some Timberland boots, they leave out the back exit and hop in his Range Rover. After driving for about 20-25 minutes they pull up to an old airstrip where a small private passenger plane awaited them.

"I thought we were going to eat?" Candy asked curiously.

"We are. Where did you think I was going to take you, to I-Hop or the Waffle House or something?" answered Snake with a chuckle of confidence that could be confused with arrogance.

"So where are we going?" inquired Candy.

"Sylvia's Chicken and Waffles in St. Louis," declared Snake.

"Oh! Wow! You on that? Ok, I'm game," expressed Candy who was quite impressed with Snake's initiative to woo her.

They boarded the small aircraft that was staffed with a pilot, co-pilot and female flight attendant. They strapped on their seatbelts and taxied down the runway. Once airborne and level, the attendant brought over a chilled bottle of champagne and two glasses. She filled the two glasses and went to have a seat in the very front of the plane, giving the two passengers privacy. Candy started the conversation after Snake proposed a toast to new beginnings.

"I bet you got this plane on standby for all your ladies, huh Snake?" she said.

"No, this is actually my first time using their services. A friend told me about it a while back, but I was saving something like this for someone special," Snake responded.

"So you think I'm special?" she asked batting her eyelashes coquettishly.

"Candy, I've had my eye on you for a little while now. I like how you carry yourself. You're not like the typical woman that I've been coming across down here. I like your lady-like swag but you can handle yourself too. I've peeped how you handle costumers that get too fly, you *get hood* right back at *'em*, but still keep it professional," Snake informed her.

"Oh, Ok! You've done your homework but are you sure you're ready for this class? See I got to be the one and only, I don't vie for position in a man's dating circle. You feel me? I'm one of those "all in" type of women. Either you throw all the chips in or fold *ya* hand!" She said as her buzz kicked in from the costly bottle of bubbly.

"I think I can handle that as long as you can walk as good a game as you talk. I cater to my woman and I like to be catered to. Now do you think you can handle that Ms. Candy?" He fired back at her.

"I wouldn't be here with you if you didn't already know the answer to that question," she replied and took another sip of her drink as they stared into each other's eyes.

The flight only took an hour and when they landed a limo was waiting to take them to the eatery. They enjoyed the signature dish at Sylvia's and returned to the private plane, via the limousine. The plane ride home was a surreal, Kush smoked filled voyage that put the finishing touches on an evening that would remain stamped in their memories forever.

Chapter 7

Verdale's cellphone rings as he enters the Greater Cincinnati Airport. "What's up?" He answers.

"What's good O.G.?" E-Tone replies.

"You tell me!" Verdale responds.

"We should be putting the icing on the cake real soon. I'll keep you posted on it, but the cake is almost finished baking," says E-Tone speaking in code.

"That's what's up. It should be one hell of a party. Y'all need any funds on the decorations, just let me know," Verdale responds in their coded lingo.

"We cool for now, but I'll let you know...I'll holla!" E-Tone says before hanging up.

Verdale smiles as he puts his cellphone away and heads toward the check-in counter. He hands the woman at the counter his ticket and I.D.

"One round trip ticket to Las Vegas, Mr. Lewis," the check-in attendant says while typing on the computer. She continues with small talk while still entering information. "Is this business or pleasure?" she says, not bothering to look up from the monitor.

Verdale forced himself to say "pleasure, just doing a little gambling".

Even though he was not interested in the casino activities whatsoever. He was going to talk to his homeboy Flash face to face. They were in too deep to discuss shipments over the airwaves.

"Your plane leaves at 9:30a.m. from terminal four and your departure time is Tuesday at 10p.m. Be sure to arrive at the Las Vegas airport an hour early due to TSA security procedures. You have a nice flight and enjoy yourself Mr. Lewis," the attendant says with a smile, while handing Verdale his boarding pass and flight itinerary.

"Thank you, enjoy your day", he replies as he takes his paperwork and ID back.

The plane ride was pleasant and uneventful. He exited the aircraft and made his way to the Enterprise Rent-A-Car hub to pick up his rental. The Dodge Charger was nice but Verdale was unimpressed with the lack of leg room the sports car had compared to the luxury SUV he typically drove. He arrived at Caesars Palace Hotel and Casino and checked into his room. Verdale had frequented many hotels, but he was always impressed with the rooms at Caesars Palace, simply because of the elegance of the furnishings.

He left the mid-west at 9:30a.m. and because of the time difference, it was only 10:30a.m. in Las Vegas, so he decided to take a nap. He set his phone to West Coast time, then set the alarm to wake him at 1:00p.m. in order to be on time for his 2:00p.m. meeting with Flash.

At 1 o'clock he awakens, showers, gets dressed and heads to the rendezvous point. He pulls into Gavizzios Italian Restaurant's parking lot. He instantly notices the yellow Lamborghini parked in front of the restaurant...one of Flash's signature gestures no doubt.

Flash was nicknamed back in college for two reasons. One being his incredible speed as a member of the Toledo track team with Verdale. Second was because of his attention grabbing clothes, cars and antics.

Verdale parks next to the Lamborghini, gets out of the vehicle and heads into the restaurant. When he enters, he is greeted by the Maître D. He gives the gentleman his name and is escorted to a private dining room where Flash greets him.

"Hola, mi hermano," Flash says in Spanish.

"What's good my guy" Verdale responds and they greet each other with a brotherly hug.

"So, what do I owe the pleasure of this meeting my friend?" Flash says as he starts the conversation.

"Look at you, enough with the small-talk huh! You know me too well!" Verdale says with a chuckle.

"You don't spend four years of your life with someone without getting to know them and I know you my friend. You wouldn't have wanted to talk to me alone without the wives and kids if it wasn't some important business. Am I right?" Flash poses the question already knowing the answer.

"Of course, you're right. You know me all too well, my friend", a smiling Verdale says. Verdale continues by saying, "let's eat and discuss an expansion opportunity".

The two sat down and ordered their meals. Verdale ordered the chicken fettuccine and Flash ordered the shrimp linguine. They exchanged small talk about their families and the old days in college while eating salad, garlic bread and drinking wine, until the main course arrived.

Verdale began, "things have been moving well in my region and I have a couple of trustworthy comrades on the team that want to relocate to the Atlanta area. The only reason that I would even consider an expansion is because these are homeboys that have been down since day one. We already have substantial players out of Atlanta and Charlotte who come up North to cop from us. We could continue to supply them as well as tap into the Florida and Alabama markets. Now the move would be an expansion because we want to keep the current hubs and just add the new Atlanta hub once the appropriate research and Facebook is done.

The expansion could mean an additional 200 bricks being moved a month, once we solidify the contacts in Florida and Alabama. I just wanted to give you the heads up on what I have planned and to simply make sure that its's a viable option. What do you think?"

"I see my friend. It sounds like you've done your homework and once you work out the details it sounds like a lucrative venture for us all. However you will have to assume some of the risk. I'll continue to ship the 250 kilos a month to the current hubs, but you will have to pay for the other 200 kilos upon delivery. Of course the total price of each brick will drop from $15,000 a piece to $12,500 a piece, does that sound fair?" asked Flash.

"Let me do the math on that real quick", Verdale says as he hits the calculator function on his cellphone. "That will be $2.5 million and the other 250 kilos will drop in price too... I think we got a deal my guy! Let me work out the kinks and we'll be making that happen real soon. Let's count on early April, May at the latest if all things go as planned" Verdale announces, and he proposes a toast, "To the future, my friend," And they clink glasses.

After finishing the meal the two men leave in the Lamborghini for a few hours of *mobbin'* around the city. The two return right before dusk to the restaurant parking lot, so

Verdale could pick up his rental car. They agree to meet in the casino lobby in a couple of hours to catch a boxing match and the after party. The two college friends enjoy an overdue, eventful weekend filled with boxing matches, comedy shows and magic shows. Tuesday evening came before they knew it and the two old friends were headed back to their respective cities with anticipation of more dollar signs in both of their eyes.

Chapter 8

"Chow!" yells the C.O. and a sea of blue moves thru the A1 dormitory aisles, like a timely tidal wave heading towards the front door.

"You coming to chow Tez?" asked Daryl, one of Vontez's homeboys from the city.

"What they servin'?" Vontez responded with a question himself.

"I think spaghetti," responds Daryl.

"Naw, I'm good. I'll make me a break later. I'm about to use the phone, while it is some peace and quiet in here. I'll meet you on the yard when I'm done," states Vontez.

"Bet," says Daryl as he heads to the door to go to the chow-hall.

Vontez makes his phone calls, but is only able to talk to one of his four children, Vonesha, his oldest daughter. He inquires about her overall well-being, health, school and social life. Pleased with her responses, they both express how much they love and miss each other and end their phone call.

Vontez had four children with four different women. Vonesha was the oldest at 13 years old, followed by Lashay at 11 years old, Vontez Jr. at 8 years old and the baby Trinity, at 6 years old. Because of Vontez's charismatic personality but unwillingness to commit whole-heartedly, he went thru a myriad of unfulfilling relationships. The children were the best thing to result from the plethora of flings, and oh how Vontez loved and spoiled his children!

After unsuccessfully trying to contact his other offspring, Vontez puts on a blue sweat suit and skull cap and heads out to the prison yard. It was the first week in November and the landscape looking away from the penitentiary was awesome. The multitude of colors, as the leaves of the trees changed from a vibrant healthy green to the oranges, yellows, reds and browns of the fall foliage was truly a spectacle.

Vontez spotted his homeboy Daryl standing with a group of guys along the walkway in front of B-Unit. He walks over by the men, gives a couple of head nods and fist bumps as greetings and the two men walk off from the crowd down to the track. Vontez very rarely ever hung in groups of more than 3 or 4 while incarcerated.

Because of his stature and prominence in the drug game, Vontez was a living legend amongst the mid-level hustlas locked up within the state facility. He only hung around crew members from his own syndicate, who happened to be housed at the same institution. Usually a dealer on his level would be doing Fed time. But because of the amount he had been caught with in his possession, which was 2 kilos, he was being warehoused in a state penitentiary. Many guys tried to get in his good graces offering to shank someone for him or commit other heinous acts of violence, just to show him what kind of asset they could be to his team. Others tried to befriend him in hopes of being put on in the game, once they were released. It seemed like everybody had an angle, except the men he had already entrusted as part of his crew from the outside.

Since Daryl and him were in the same dorm, they spent a lot of time *politicking* together. Daryl was doing 8 years for aggravated drug trafficking. He had got caught with one brick and a pistol but because of his past record, he had received a stiff sentence. He had been down for over 5 years. Three of which was mandatory because of the gun specification. With less than three years left, he and Vontez were due home around the same time. Daryl never wanted for anything while he was down. Vontez made sure that anybody in the crew that went down and kept their lips sealed were handsomely rewarded with the same loyalty.

Vontez started the conversation, "Man, I'm salty. I only got to talk to one of my kids. They know I call every

Saturday, they Mamas probably on some bullshit. I did get to talk to Vonesha though, wit her grown butt."

Vontez started the conversation, "Man, I'm salty. I only got to talk to one of my kids. They know I call every Saturday, they Mamas probably on some bullshit. I did get to talk to Vonesha though, wit her grown butt."

"Oh, yeah! How's she doing?" says Daryl.

"Oh, she good. Thanks for asking Homie. What's been good with you? Since you on the 2nd shift porter crew, we don't get to kick it like we used to," states Vontez.

"I know! I be tired as fuck during the day usually. I guess my body is still adjusting. I did get a letter from my little brother "Turtle", the other day. He up in London Correctional Institution now. He got 2 years to do but between the county, CRC and a little over a month at London, he got 6 months in already, but he said his girl done jumped out the whip already," Daryl said.

"Damn, already. That bitch ain't got no loyalty at all!" comments Vontez.

"I told him that most chicks in the city ain't built for this prison shit.   I can tell it got him fucked up, up there. I can feel his pain in the letter. On top of that, he left her his whip and some money and the car is in her name, so he ain't *gettin'* that shit back," remarks Daryl.

"Damn, that's fucked up!" interjects Vontez.

"I know, I don't think he left her all his lil chips, but he did leave her a few bands. I told him don't let that shit stress him out too bad, but this his first rodeo. So, I know it's hitting him hard. But the shit ain't *gonna* kill 'em, only makes his ass stronger so it is what it is!" acknowledges Daryl.

"Yeah, sometimes the best life lessons can be the most painful. He'll be alright, especially when he come home *eatin'* like a fat rat and karma done caught up with that bitch!" states Vontez.

"What's up with the Snake situation, did the homies rock his ass to sleep yet?" asked Daryl.

"Naw, not yet. You know how E-Tone and J.J. work. They gone bleed his ass dry before they put the pitchfork in his ass!" and both the men laughed sinisterly.

Chapter 9

It had been over three weeks since Candy and Snake had started dating and they had become pretty much inseparable, much like Sapphire and Jerome. Both cousins had invited their respective girls to Thanksgiving Dinner at Jerome's mother's house with the rest of the Collins/Erving clan. Both Sapphire and Candy were eager to meet the family on Thanksgiving, but for different reasons. Candy was excited because she had genuine affection for Jerome and wanted to meet the woman who had molded her man into the perfect, kind and loving gentleman that he was. Candy knew that by being invited to Thanksgiving dinner to meet Snake's family that he was developing deep feelings for her and that was working to her advantage.......towards her ultimate goal.

Since their involvement Sapphire no longer danced at the club. She and Jerome were pretty much attached at the hip and very rarely did you see one without the other. Candy however, still worked as a bartender at the club, although her and Snake were a serious item. While off the clock, Snake had expressed to Candy that she no longer had to work because she was his woman, but Candy wanted to maintain her independent façade. Both of the women had told a collaborative story of their financial aid not coming through, and that was the reason why they weren't attending school this semester. Unbeknownst to Sapphire, Jerome had every intention of paying for her to complete her education.

Candy rolled over to answer a text message on her phone. The text message was from Sapphire and reads, "Happy Thanksgiving sweetie! See you later at Jerome's Mamas house XOXO."

Candy looks at the text and the date says 11-27- 14. She thinks to herself that a lot has changed in her life the past couple of months. What started off as a simple assignment had turned into a much more intricate situation. Although she had told Sapphire numerous times not to fall in love with Jerome, she herself, was liking the company, conversation and caress of Snake way too much. She had to remember he was the target.

Before she could return to her snoozing, her phone rang. She looks up at the screen and a picture of Snake pops up. She answers, "good morning boo! Did you make it back safely?"

"Good morning beautiful I'm pulling into the city as we speak. Are we still on for the Thanksgiving dinner at my aunt's house or are you nervous?" he playfully asked.

"You silly, of course we still on plus my girl going to be there too so I'm good. Did you want me to drive over your house and we leave from there or do you want to pick me up?" asked Candy.

"It's up to you baby girl," he states.

"I'll come over and get dressed. What color scheme are we wearing? I know how you like to c-o-o-r-d-i-n-a-t-e!" She laughs at her own joke of stretching her words like comedian John Witherspoon.

"Oh, you got jokes this morning. Why don't you throw something on and head over now. Don't worry about no clothes, I got you a few outfits to choose from, funny lady," Snake says with playful sarcasm. "Plus, I have a sweet tooth this morning. I'm in need of some Candy."

"Boy what are you trying to do to me, get me dick-whipped or something," she teasingly replies.

"Hell are you on your way?" Snake quickly retorts.

"Of course," she responds.

"See you in a minute babe," he says.

She hangs up and heads to the bathroom to get showered. When she arrives at Snake's home, in the gated community of Wellington Estates, the guard at the entrance stops the vehicle to write down the license plate before allowing her admittance. This formality was something Candy had grown accustomed to.

"Hello Miss. Sinclair," the scrawny guard greets Candy, as he checks her name off the approved visitors list.

"Good morning Colin and Happy Thanksgiving to you," she replies as he opened the sliding black gates.

"Happy Thanksgiving to you too," he manages to say before Candy pulls off into the complex of expensive homes.

After a left, then a right turn, Candy makes another right into Snake's wide driveway that led to a three-car garage. While Snake was getting undressed, he noticed on his security camera Candy's black Camry in the driveway. He watched her get out of the car and walk up to the front door before hitting the intercom button.

As he pressed the door buzzer unlocking his front door he said, "Baby come on in, I'm upstairs in the bedroom!"

She answered, "Okay", before entering his immaculate living quarters.

The room was filled with soothing and calming earth tones picked out by Snake's interior decorator.

Candy went upstairs entering the bedroom only to find it empty. The bathroom door was ajar and she could hear the stream of water beating against the sliding shower door. She announced herself as she entered the bathroom.

"Hey baby can I join you?" she asked already slipping out of the sweat shirt and yoga pants she had thrown on.

Snake remained silent, sliding the shower door open and stepping back allowing her full access to enter. "This is going to be one of the best Thanksgivings I've had in a long time," he said.

"Why is that baby," she asked as she entered and closed the shower door. Taking the bar of soap from his hand she stood behind him lathering up his muscular back.

"Because I have a lot to be thankful for; business is going good, the club is flourishing and now I have you! My mother would've loved you!" he remarked as he thought about his mother's untimely death due to cancer a couple of years ago. He continues, "She always wanted me to settle down with a pretty girl and give her some grandbabies. I was too busy ripping and running the streets trying to come up to focus on the simpler things in life -- that is until I found you Candy-Cane!" He turned around facing Candy, to see her tearing up. He lifted her chin to stare into her watering eyes. "What's wrong babe?" he inquisitively asks.

"I just never expected to have these deep feelings for you so fast. I love the way I feel when I'm in your presence," she managed to say thru her whimpering, partially revealing the truth. But the underlying reason was her guilt, having agreed to conspire to kill the man she had grown to love, undeniably.

"Baby you don't have to cry no more, you're with me now and I'm going to take care of you. I ain't going nowhere

Candy-Cane!" Snake confidently says, unaware of the devious plot in play against him.

They kiss fervently with Snake gently nibbling on Candy's bottom lip, something that he learned, turned her on instantaneously. The tongue wrestling ceased when Snake moved his head downward. He found Candy's hardened-by-stimulation nipples on the end of her perky and firm "B" cup breasts. He sucked and passionately kissed her titties, while he inserted one, then two fingers into her damp love cave. Candy moaned and groaned in pleasure, as Snake methodically stroked and strummed in and out of her moist pussy, each time lightly brushing against her clitoris. Snake reveled in pleasing his new love, Candy-Cane.

Before she could cum Candy removed Snake's two saturated digits and seductively sucked the sticky fluid off of them and turned around to face the back wall of the shower. She put her right leg on the edge of the tub and grabbed the towel bar in front of her and tooted her ass in the air, allowing ample access to Snake's stiffened curved extremity. He instinctively entered her breeding ground grabbing her small waist at the base of her widening hips. With each stroke he gained deeper entry into what felt like a physical paradise, from which he never wanted to escape. And with each stroke, Candy's emotions changed from deep feelings to a solidified love, something she had assured herself wouldn't happen.

Candy turned her head over her left shoulder and said, "Pernell Collins I love you! *I'm cummin'* baby!"

Before exploding inside of her he shouted, "I love you too Candice Sinclair! Ooh I'm *cummin'* too Baby girl!"

The two climaxed together, satisfying carnal desires that lived inside of them both. They finished showering and went to the bedroom to get dressed.

Snake opened the walk-in closet on the opposite side of the room from where his closet was located. New outfits lined half the length of the 12ft closet. Shoeboxes lined the top shelf and panty and bra sets were grouped together on the far end. Candy was flabbergasted by his outward show of affection.

"Oh my God Baby!! You are too much! Here it is Thanksgiving and you spoiling me like its Christmas. Thank you so much, I love you Nell!" she exuberantly proclaimed and gave him a melodramatic kiss.

"I told you Candy-Cane, you're with me now Baby. You ain't got to worry about nothing, I got you on whatever!" he told her with sincerity in his voice.

They got dressed in matching outfits. Candy picked out a cream colored, form fitting wrap around sweater dress with some knee high, brown stiletto boots, brown bangle bracelets and matching necklace to accessorize. Snake wore a cream colored Polo sweater, brown True Religion jeans and some brown Kenneth Cole boots. After Candy applied minimal make-up, they stood side by side in the mirror admiring how well they complimented each other. Once they were gratified with their self-observation, they made their way downstairs.

Snake stopped in the kitchen and grabbed the keys to the 2013 760 BMW because it coordinated with their outfits, being pearl white with saddle-colored interior, and headed toward his aunt's house. They pulled up to see a cluster of cars in the driveway in front of the house and on the sidewalk and grass in front of the house. Jerome's 5500 Benz was included amongst them.

Jerome's mother had a large older home on the Westside of the city. It was the same residence that Jerome grew up in and the same house where Snake stayed, during his summertime visits to Louisville. After finding a parking space down the street from the house, they got out of the Beamer and walked up to the front door. They entered through the unlocked door to find the entire Collins/Erving clan present.

The clan included Jerome's mother and father, his three sisters, their husbands and children. As well as two of Jerome's uncles on his father's side, their wives and a couple of their grown children and their grandkids. Also in the clan was one widowed aunt on his father's side, one of her adult sons and his wife and two little boys. Snakes two half-sisters and their kids were present too. One was a single mother and the other one's husband was there also.

Jerome's mother and Snake's father were brother and sister. Snake was his incarcerated father's only son and was his spitting image. Snake's father, Pernell Collins, Sr. had received a life sentence for a murder in the late 1980's in Louisville. Jerome's mother, Odessa, had made it her business to stay in contact with her brother's only son. When his mother moved him from Louisville to Cincinnati, his aunt sent for him every summer during his adolescent and early teen years. This was before Snake was introduced to the street life.

On this day, everyone was in a festive mood. The adults were making introductions to the new family friends and catching up on current events in the lives of their relatives. The children were playing Ping Pong and other board games in the finished basement. Jerome and Snake's sisters were giving Candy and Sapphire a light-hearted grilling, in an inquisitive but playful manner. Mrs. Odessa and the older women were doing last minute preparation to the meal in the kitchen.

Jerome, Snake and the other men, their brothers-in-law and cousins, were drinking and smoking on the enclosed rear patio. Candy and Sapphire were enjoying the family oriented atmosphere and they were happy to be sharing the experience with one another. After about 20-30 minutes and the arrival of a few more family members, everyone was called to the dining room for the family Thanksgiving prayer.

The entire family crammed into the aroma filled room to hold hands in a circle. It was customary for each individual to share what they were thankful for this year. Jerome's father, Big Jerry, led the prayer, "Dear Heavenly Father, I want to thank you for showing us your grace and mercy through-out the year and for the health of every individual under the sound of my voice. Father your word says where two or more are gathered in prayer your presence is there and I truly feel your presence today. Father God, we ask that you bless the hands that prepared this food we are about to receive for the nourishment of our bodies. And we thank you for this opportunity to fellowship with one another in your son's name Jesus Christ we pray, Amen."

Thanksgiving speeches went around the room and when it came to Jerome to say his 'what I'm thankful for speech he cleared his throat and began with, "I have a lot to be thankful for this year, the health of my family, the flourishing business that my cousin and I are running. But I'm especially happy and thankful for my precious Sapphire." Sapphire blushes at the mention of her name. Jerome continues. "I've prayed for God to send me someone that is not only physically attractive, but mentally stimulating as well, not to mention a sweet, loving, kind and attentive God fearing woman. I've found all of these qualities in you my love," he says as he stares into Sapphire's eyes before dropping to one knee and pulling out a blue ring box with the Tiffany logo from his pants pocket. She tears up and holds her hand over her mouth in astonishment – He continues, "Baby, I've found everything that I've ever wanted in a wife in you, so I know my search is over. Sapphire Marie Turner, will you marry me?"

The entire family stood smiling and speechless. Some of the women in the Collins/Erving family were crying tears from the romantic sentiment of their brother, cousin and nephew. Jerome's Mama was weeping tears of joy with pride in her son's chivalrous gesture. What was only seconds seemed like an eternity as Sapphire pondered ever so briefly her obvious decision.

"Yes, of course I'll marry you, Romey!" she exclaimed to her future husband.

The house erupted in applause and cheers for the happy couple. They both knew this moment was coming, sooner or later! It just so happened to be sooner than later. The family continued around the room but everyone's attention was still focused on the marriage proposal. After the entire family said what they were thankful for, including the kids, family members fixed plates and sat in various parts of the house once the dining room was at capacity.

The entire family was coming over to congratulate the newly engaged couple and get a glimpse of the 3 carat Princess Cut diamond engagement ring. This was definitely a Thanksgiving to remember for the Collins/Erving Family.

Chapter 10

Thanksgiving dinner at Mama V's house was finishing up after a delicious spread was devoured by the family. The entire close-knit Lewis tribe was there, with the exception of Vontez, who was well represented at the family gathering. Stephanie and Keisha were both in attendance along with all four of Vontez's children, who were all dropped off by their respective mothers without incident. Verdale, Regina and the twins were also there of course. Mama V's brother and his wife were present, along with their son, his wife and two children. It was a small but intimate group of relatives who genuinely enjoyed each other's company. The three adult men and all of the male children were watching television in the family room.

The football game was their focus of interest. The women were going back and forth from the dining room to the kitchen putting away the left-over food and clearing dirty dishes. Mama V's house phone rings and she sees it's Vontez by the 740 area code on the caller id.

Once she accepts the call she starts up, "Boy, I thought you were *gonna* miss everybody. Why are you just now calling?"

"Happy Thanksgiving to you too Mama." Vontez says with a light hearted laugh.

"Baby, I'm sorry. Happy Thanksgiving and you know I love ya", she apologetically and affectionately replies.

"I love you too Ma! Let me talk to my girls, if you don't mind."

"Which ones? The big ones or your kids?" she playfully asks.

"You silly Ma. I'll talk to Stephanie and Keisha after I've talked to the kids. Y'all still going Black Friday shopping?"

"You know it. We're *gonna* head out in a couple of hours. Vonesha *gonna* babysit while we're out. Hold on let me get *yo'* kids in here; Nesha, Shay, Lil Tez and Trinity y'all daddy on the phone."

The girls come running first, followed by their brother who was still peeking his head in the family room trying to catch Dallas' scoring drive.

"Hi Daddy!! Happy Thanksgiving!" The girls say in unison on the speaker phone.

"How y'all doing young ladies? I miss y'all so much."

"We miss you too Daddy," the girls respond.

"Vonesha chimes in, "Daddy are we still doing the video visit on Christmas?"

"Of course we are Baby. Did you guys give Grandma V y'all Christmas list?" he asked his girls.

"Yes sir!" They answered on one accord.

"Where y'all brother at?"

Hearing his daddy mention his name, Lil Tez comes from the doorway of the TV/Family room to answer. "I'm right here Daddy. What's up?"

"What's up? Fo'real Junior? That's how you talking now son?" he asked in a fatherly playful tone.

"My bad Daddy."

"Naw, I'm just playing son, I see you got *yo*'swag up!"

"I wanna be like you Daddy when I grow up, two girlfriends and everything".

The girls giggle at their brother's comment.

"Oh yeah? Just like me huh?"

"Yes sir, just like you!" his son says smiling from ear to ear.

"Well son, I want you to be better than me. I want you to be on T.V. playing football on Thanksgiving when you get big. How's that sound?" Vontez asks his son.

His 8 year old responds, "I think I can handle that Daddy. I had 13 touchdowns this year in Pop Warner and I was voted the MVP, and I've been doing my push-ups every night like you told me. And I've been eating all my vegetables and drinking milk."

"Wow, ok. I knew you were having a good year, but I didn't know that you ended the season with that many touchdowns. Thirteen touchdowns in a 6 game season, that's incredible son! I'm really proud of you!"

"Thanks Daddy!" his son says emphatically.

He finishes his conversation with his children before the 15 minute prison phone call ends. He tells his children how he loves them and misses them and that he would talk to them real soon. Vontez never received visits from his kids, not be *'cause* they didn't want to see him, but because he didn't want them to experience the humiliating visiting procedures of the prison. Vontez got back in line for the phone a couple more times that Thanksgiving Day. The second time he called his brother's cellphone, to talk about the new business expansion down south, in code of course and the 3rd time he called Stephanie's cellphone to talk to her and Keisha about filling his children's Christmas list order. He also wished them a happy holiday and inquired about their upcoming scheduled visit. After talking to everyone Vontez went back to his rack to finish eating a penitentiary pizza he had made earlier.

The girls, Stephanie and Keisha, finish helping Mama V put away the food and helped her clean the dining room and kitchen. Mama V, Regina, Stephanie, Keisha, Mama V's Sister-in-law and her daughter-in-law all piled up in two vehicles headed for the outlet mall. Mama V in her SRX and Regina, Stephanie and Keisha rode in the black BMW X5 that they had rode in together to the Thanksgiving dinner. They rode up I-75 to the Lebanon/Monroe exit to the outlet mall, with Mama V leading the way.

"Girl, y'all gone have me smelling like them tweeds y'all smoking. Mama V gone have a fit," Gina said as Stephanie passed Keisha the lit Kush blunt as she drove up the expressway.

"Don't worry *Boo Thang*, we got some body spray for ya!" Stephanie said with smoke coming out of her nostrils

"Shit, Mama V probably *gonna* be salty 'cause she ain't get to hit this *muthafucka*, but she got her sister and niece-in-law tagging along," Keisha said after inhaling the thick smoke.

"You ain't never smoked wit Dale and his Mama *Miss Thang*?" Stephanie jokingly asked Regina.

"Girl, I ain't smoked since college, the shit just make me sleepy honestly, but I didn't know Mama V got down. She a trip," Gina replied with naiveté.

"Girl Mama V probably can out smoke us both, on some real shit!" Keisha chimed in.

"I know that's right," added Stephanie.

"Anyway let us know when you and Dale need us to watch the twins for y'all, you know we family now," Keisha said changing the subject.

"I don't mean to be nosey, but girl how does that work with y'all? I mean I know how it works, I ain't stupid but emotionally how does it work for y'all both to share Tez?" Regina asked posing the question to no one in particular.

Stephanie commented first, "Baby girl we a team. Keisha my Boo and Vontez is my Boo."

Keisha added, "We all have each other's back and don't think Tez is the only one having his cake and eating it too. Shit we got the best of both worlds over here." She leaned over and tongue kissed Stephanie for added emphasis to make her point loud and clear.

Stephanie continued, "We ain't got to worry about him cheating on us, we all are satisfied completely."

"Girl that's what's up. If y'all like it then I love it. I couldn't share Dale, I'd cut a bitch over his ass!" Gina remarked with her voice changing from prissy to semi-gangsta.

"I heard that shit!" Stephanie said.

Keisha added, "I see the princess got a lil hood in her. She must be getting a contact or something."

The three women laughed together as they arrived at the outlet mall and hit the stores in their mini entourage with Mama V leading the charge with her motherly sarcastic wit. The shopping spree was filled with gaiety and laughter and all of the women had a ball purchasing gifts for their loved ones.

Chapter 11

It was a beautiful, chilly Sunday morning and both Sapphire and Candy found themselves at their condo for the first time in what seemed like weeks. Both girls were back at their residence preparing for Sunday service with the Collins/Erving family at Ebenezer Baptist Church.

"Girl, you going to church this morning?" asked Sapphire.

"Yeah, I wanted to show off my black Coach purse. It seems more appropriate for church. But Sapphire girl, I'm so happy for you and Jerome! I know I said not to fall in love, buy y'all look so happy and cute together. Additionally, his family is so nice and loving. I've never had a Thanksgiving dinner like that in my life and it was so romantic how he proposed to you. I was in tears Girl!" Candy expressed with joy for her closest friend.

"Candy I know. I feel like this whole situation is like a fairy-tale and both of us are princesses. You and Snake look like y'all were made for each other and I can tell you got feelings for him by the way you beam with delight when you're around him. Plus you can't help but to see the love he has for you by the way he looks at you," Sapphire declares.

"Girl, I know but we got this damn scheme going on. I don't think I can go through with it. I mean you're good *'cause* Jerome ain't the main target no way. But I don't know how to get thru to E-Tone and J.J., them niggas don't know how to turn down. If I tell them how I feel about Snake, those niggas will kill me and you to cover up their tracks. I'm scared to tell Snake, because how do you tell a *muthafucka* that I was sent here to set you up but I wound up falling in love with you. Girl, I'm so torn I don't know what to do. I love him too much to let anything happen to him. But if we don't go through with the plan, then we both are in for it," says a visibly distraught Candy.

"Listen Candy, we *gonna* figure this out. Have you heard from them niggas since they gave us the bill money?" Sapphire asked Candy.

"No, but I know E-Tone will be texting me for an update any day now. Plus me and Snake was pillow talking last night after we made love. I guess he was feeling guilty about some stuff and wanted to get it off of his chest. He said that he had made some mistakes in the game and he was ashamed of himself. He explained that he knew his mother's cancer had spread and he knew that she had a year or less to live when he caught a case. He said that the arresting agents knew his dilemma and used it against him. They told him that if he didn't cooperate that he would never see his mother alive again, unless it was thru the thick county glass jail. That is when they told him that they didn't want him fo'real but they wanted his connect. He was his mother's only child and he felt like he had no choice.

He said he set *"the connect"* up for the least amount he could, which was two bricks because dude was always fair with him. He also said that in order for him not to receive any jail time he had to agree to relocate and work with them in the future and that's something he can't stomach to do anymore. He says he just wants a simple life with me and maybe a couple of kids. Maybe the only way for us all to be safe is to just leave and start over somewhere under aliases. All four of us," Candy emphatically said in a tone of desperation.

"Girl, let's go to church and pray on it. Jerome's picking me up any minute. Are you *gonna* ride with us?" Sapphire asked.

"No, I just came to grab this purse. I'm about to head back over to his place and ride there with him. I'll see y'all there," replied Candy

"Girl don't worry. It's *gonna* work itself out. We deserve to be happy. God ain't *gonna* let these good men come into our lives for Him to just take them away. Shit, I'm tired of being used. I finally got the opportunity to be treated right for a change and I ain't giving this up without a fight.

You hear me? I love you girl. I'll see you in a minute," Sapphire announced as Candy was standing by the front door.

"I love you too and we do deserve to be happy for a change. It's time for us to start thinking about our future. I'm so cool on the life we were used to living!" Candy retorted and the girls embraced before Candy left.

When Snake and Candy pulled up to the massive church structure, Candy was thoroughly impressed after taking in the beautiful granite and glass architecture outside. The splendor of the artistically decorated sanctuary inside of the church was magnificent. Snake greeted a couple of the ushers with a handshake before entering the sanctuary arm-in- arm with Candy.

Candy scanned the congregation and recognized a few of the family members from the Thanksgiving dinner. She spotted Sapphire and Jerome on the left side toward the middle of a pew. The couple acknowledged family members by waving at them as they made their way to sit by Sapphire and Jerome. The cousins gave each other dap and the women hugged and kissed each other on the cheek. The cousins gave each other's woman an innocent hug before they all sat down to hear the service.

The captivating choir sang an array of hymns ranging from classic to contemporary. One of the younger female relatives was a member of the choir and this made the family proud. After a few announcements were made about who was in need of prayer and reminders about the church building fund, the Pastor began to preach.

"Good morning God's people," he began and the congregation responded' "Good Morning," in a lack luster tone.

"I know y'all can do better than that! I said good morning!"

The congregation responded again for a second time sounding more fired up this time.

"I hope that everybody had a wonderful Thanksgiving meal and enjoyed the company of their loved ones. We need to savor those precious moments that we get to spend with our family and friends because nothing is promised to us. The only thing that is truly promised to us is to meet our maker one day, and when our time comes you need to have your life right with God. Nobody knows when that final hour will be upon you. That's why I urge you today to make some changes in your life while you have the chance. Those of you who haven't given your life to Christ might think that you are not good enough or worthy to get into heaven or not righteous enough to receive salvation. Well I'm here to give you that chance. Once you give your life to Christ, your past doesn't matter. That old life of yours is just that, your old life.

The Bible says in 2 Corinthians 5:17, *"Therefore, if anyone is in Christ, the new creation has come. The old has gone, the new is here!"* Let me translate the text for you. Once you accept Jesus Christ as your Lord and Savior, then you have become a new person, just as simple as that! Your past is something that is behind you as long as you move forward in life and don't look back, you'll never see your past again. And let me tell you something, when you change who you are, people are going to take notice. Some of your old friends are going to wonder why you don't do the things you used to do. Some of your old hanging buddies are going to notice that you don't hang where you use to hang or go to some of the places you use to go. I'm telling you that people are going to look at you different. When you stop talking how you used to talk, when you stop doing the thangs you used to do, people are going to take notice. I think I'm *preachin'* better than y'all listening. Can I get an Amen?" The church crowd responded with an astounding Amen.

The reverend continues, "The Bible says in Ephesians 2:8-9 that "*by grace you have been saved, through faith and that not of yourselves. It is the gift of God not of works, lest anyone should boast.*" Now let me break that down for you. There is nothing that you can physically do to get into heaven, but God gives us the precious gift of grace and underserving grace might I add, because of faith. The faith of receiving salvation by accepting His only begotten son Jesus Christ as our Lord and Savior. John 3:16 says "*for God so loved the world that He gave His one and only son. That whoever believes in him shall not perish but have eternal life.*" Jesus, who was without sin gave his life for our sins. His sacrifice paid the price for those who believe in Him. Can I get an Amen?"

The church responds in a multitude of Amens. Reverend Thompson preached an awesome stirring sermon that beautiful Sunday morning. When he got to the end of the service, before offering the benediction, he asked the congregation as always, "Is there anybody under the sound of my voice, who doesn't know Jesus Christ as your Lord and Savior and you're ready to make that change in your earthly life, in order to receive eternal salvation? I ask that you make your way to the front of the church. Is there anybody who's tired of living the life you've been living and is ready to turn over a new leaf? I want you to walk down that aisle and come to the front of this church, in the name of Jesus."

Sapphire and Candy, who had both been emotional during the stimulating service, looked at each other thru teary eyes and grabbed each other's hand, stood up and made their way to the front. That morning both of the girls were saved in front of the congregation, which included the men in their lives, as well as their family.

Chapter 12

"Damn these hoes on some deep cover shit. Coming to church and every *muthafuckin'* thing." J.J. says to E-Tone as they sat down the street from Ebenezer Baptist Church.

They had been doing their own reconnaissance that Sunday morning. Following Candy when she left her condo to Snake's gated community home and then to church when they left the iron fortress of a community.

"Yeah, I know. I was wondering why these bitches don't keep me posted like they used to, bout shit! If it was just about killing this punk ass nigga we could've been slumped his ass, but we got to get that paper too." E-Tone diabolically says to J.J.

"Shit, *sho* you right! If it don't make dollaz, then it don't make sense, my nigga!" replies J.J.

"Hell yeah, we got too much time and money invested in this *muthafuckin'* mission and I ain't *gonna* let these love-sick hoes fuck it up for us. On some real shit, we already know this nigga's schedule and shit. We just need Candy's ass to let us know when he sitting on full and to get us past the guard at the front gate if he keep his shit there," E-Tone says as if he's thinking out loud. He continued, "I'm *gonna* have to check them hoes pulse later on and that's my word, Homie!"

The two left the scene keeping a low profile in the black Lincoln MKZ with tinted windows.

Meanwhile back in Cincinnati......

Verdale's cellphone rings and he answers, "What's up, Sweet Lou?"

"You know me, Young Blood, fair for a square. I'm sitting here with Spiller and we talked to your brother yesterday. He said you might be interested in going to the College All-star game with us, since he can't come of course. What you think, Lil Dale?" (Sweet Lou and Spiller were Vontez's business partners in My Brother's Keeper Sports Agency also known as "MBK".

"I always did wanna check one of those events out, shit when is it?" asked Verdale.

"It's this Saturday, but we're leaving out on Tuesday, we got a couple of prospects we're looking at. Can you make it on such short notice?" Louis asked with concern.

"I ain't got too much going on this week, I'm *gonna* okay it with the wife just to be considerate, but we should be cool," an excited Verdale responded.

"Cool, call me back later to confirm, that way I can finalize the particulars with you," said Louis.

"Bet. Talk to you later Big Homies," Verdale said before hanging up the phone.

After informing his wife Regina of his plans and receiving her approval, Verdale confirms with Louis and Bernard and the trio were all set for Tuesday's departure.

Tuesday morning Verdale met Louis and Bernard at Greater Cincinnati Airport bright and early around 9:00. They had a 10:00a.m. flight headed for Tempe, Arizona. It had been a couple of years since they had seen each other. Verdale considered his brother's ex-teammates and current business partners like two older brothers. As Dale walks up to Terminal 4, he sees his two travel companions awaiting his arrival.

"What's up fellas?" he says as the two men stood up to greet him with brotherly love.

"Look at this Renaldo Niemiah built Nigga; Boy you ain't *gonna* never gain no weight," Spiller says, with his signature big smile as he bear hugs Dale.

"Boy you still slim and trim. We might have to sign you as a split end or flanker for somebody, as good of shape as you're in," Louis states jokingly as he daps and hugs Verdale.

"That might be over now that I've been squeezed to death by Warren Sapp and Reggie White!" Dale says wisecracking as he readjusts his clothes.

The three men share a hearty laugh together after checking in with the ticket agent. Shortly afterwards the men board the plane. It was a smooth and relaxing journey to the West and once they arrived, the weather was stellar. The three friends checked into their room at the "W" Luxury Hotel and made plans to meet in the lobby in an hour.

The view from the 25th floor of the hotel was breathtaking. Arizona, although it was early December, looked and felt like an early summer day. The men took the rental SUV to the stadium where the East-West College All-star game practices were being held. Upon entering the stadium and making their way to the sideline to get a closer look at the pre-professional players, the men run into an old friend from college, Lamont Green. He was a former running back on their Toledo football team who had torn his MCL and ACL during their senior year, which crushed his dreams of turning pro. The light skinned, stocky guy could have passed for Mack 10's brother.

"What's up my fellow Toledo alumni? Y'all down here trying to steal some of my prospects?" Lamont jokingly asked with a smile.

"Hey, what up my dude?" Louis says as he greets him with a pound.

"What's good Homeboy? Longtime no see," says Spiller as he daps it up with their college teammate.

"It's good to see y'all too. I see y'all still hanging tight, just like the old days," expresses an exuberant Lamont.

"Hey you remember Vontez's little brother Verdale?" Spiller asks as he reacquaints the two men.

"Yeah, I remember Lil Dale. What's up man, how you been?" he asked.

"I'm good, thanks for asking. How about you?" Verdale replies.

"I'm making it down here, *tryin'* to get another meal ticket out of this bunch of young bucks," Lamont says with a quipping tone. He continues to say, "Hey, where your brother, is he here too?"

"Naw, my brother got into a little trouble a couple years back. He'll be home soon though," Verdale explains.

"I'm sorry to hear that. Tell him I said, what's up and that I'm praying for him the next time you talk to him," sincerely says Lamont.

"I sure will my brotha," retorts Verdale.

"So where y'all staying at? Maybe we can hook up and catch up on old times later?" Lamont states to the small group of men.

Louis answers, "We're at the "W" on Santa Rosa Avenue."

"Cool, I'm right down the street at the Embassy Suites. How about we meet at the Benihanas. It's on Santa Rosa too. How about 8 o'clock?"

"Sounds copasetic to me," Spiller replies.

"Cool, that's what's up. I'll see y'all then," Lamont says as he gives each one a fist bump before leaving to go look at a group of defensive backs.

The old college mates and Verdale enjoy a memorable few days scouting players by day, and enjoying the exhilarating night life of the college town of Tempe, Arizona. By the start of the game that Saturday, My Brother's Keeper (a.k.a MBK) sports agency had landed Logan Williams, a tight end out of Wake Forrest, who ended the game with 7 catches for 85 yards, 2 touchdowns and ultimately was named the All-Star Game's MVP.

Chapter 13

"Agent Erkenburger, I need to see you in my office now! I mean right now!" yells Lieutenant Madison.

"Yes sir!" says an uneasy Agent Erkenburger, who was the arresting officer in Snake's case.

"Internal Affairs is in on your ass and when they are on your ass, they are on my ass. Apparently some of the crooks you've arrested are all singing the same song about you violating their civil rights. Now, I don't give a fuck about their so-called civil rights. But what I care about is arrests and your arrests are down. We need a couple of your informants to get their heads out of their asses and set some mid to high level drug dealers up. Hell, maybe even give us some reliable information about some of the unsolved murders or something! "IA" investigations are unavoidable, so there's nothing we can do about that, but what I do know is that they are less likely to enforce disciplinary action on an agent who is bringing big dollars into the department and arrests mean dollars!" bellows Lieutenant Madison.

"I understand sir," a humbled yet relieved Agent Erkenburger says.

"Is that all sir?" asks Agent Erkenburger.

"Is that all? Get a load of this guy! Yeah, that's it for now!" says a still heated Lieutenant Madison.

Erkenburger leaves the Lieutenant's office and lets out a sigh of relief that the Internal Affairs investigation wasn't about what he thought it would be. He had been taking pure product out of the evidence room and had been replacing it with severely cut product, without detection obviously. Snake, who had complied with the terms of his plea deal, had given up a couple of high-level players in the game to complete the deal that had been struck on paper. But he and Agent Erkenburger had made an off-the-record agreement, an agreement that had been profitable for them both. But right now the agent needed his personal informant's help. Agent Erkenburger texted Snake to meet him at their regular rendezvous spot in an hour. Snake answers his request with an "okay" and the meeting was set.

The agent was waiting at the abandoned warehouse in Georgetown, KY where he and Snake would meet on occasions to exchange product, money and information. It was the halfway point on I-75 between Cincinnati and Louisville, making it convenient for both men. Snake pulled into the warehouse from the back entrance-exit and parked directly in front of the agent's all black on black 2014 Chevy Tahoe with limo tinted windows. Snake was driving his most inconspicuous vehicle, a 2012 black Chevy Impala with smoke tinted windows. Once he cut the engine he exits the car.

He begins the conversation haltingly with, "What's good guy? Your text sounded somewhat different than usual, what's the emergency? We weren't supposed to meet until the end of the month."

"I got a proposition for *ya* and you know we can't talk over these hot-ass airwaves," Guy remarks.

"Oh yeah? A proposition huh? I'm not sure if I like the sound of that. The last time I agreed to one of y'all propositions, I had to tell on my homeboy. You already know how I felt about being put between a rock and a hard place. And for the record, y'all took advantage of that shit," Snake replies bitterly.

"Well, this is a little different. I need a couple of major players or some Intel on some of these unsolved homicides in the region. I promise this is the last time for any *snitchin'* type of shit. From here on out we'll be business partners, strictly *fuckin'* with the YAYO! What'll you say Snake old buddy? Just do me this one last favor and we're good on that end," Guy says sounding sincere and a little bit desperate.

Snake scratches his head in a quandary regarding Guy's words. "So you mean to tell me that if I do you this one last favor, then I'm free and clear and you still gone plug me with the coke? Man, what's the catch?" he asked in disbelief.

"That's it straight up Snake, I swear it. I just need something solid in the next couple of weeks to get my superiors off my ass and hell, you don't even have to stay in Louisville anymore. I'll get the stuff to you wherever, if I have to mail it there myself!" Guy says with reassurance.

"The next couple of weeks huh. You *tryin'* to fuck up somebody's Christmas or better yet, you want me to fuck up somebody's Christmas. Well let me turn over a few rocks and see what's good. I'll let you know something real soon. By the way here's $150,000 on my bill, I didn't think I was going to see you for a few more weeks, but I'll be done on schedule," Snake says as he hands Agent Guy Erkenburger the black duffle bag full of cash.

"Ok, I need you to come thru for me Snake. Talk to you soon," Guy says as he pops the trunk to throw the duffle bag in it and gets in his vehicle.

Snake gives the agent a head nod as he watches him pull out of the abandoned warehouse parking lot. Snake follows suit, and exits the warehouse seconds after the agent. The whole ride back to the city of Louisville, Snake reflects on being a misfortunate ally in the agent's dilemma.

Chapter 14

The date was Sunday, December 7, 2014 and the girls had been officially saved for a week, but they were finding it difficult to keep avoiding the phone calls of E-Tone and J.J. The text messages weren't going to cut it anymore. Candy was trying to figure out the best way to tell Snake what was going on. She figured the sooner she told him, the better. Unsure of how he was going to take the news of deception, she thought it would be best if she and Sapphire sat down with the cousins together. They had attended church earlier and they were planning on having dinner at Snake's place. Candy was looking forward to showcasing her cooking skills to the man she was in love with, although she was nervous about divulging such critical and condemning information.

Snake was downstairs in the finished basement, straightening up before their company arrived. Candy was in the spacious kitchen, equipped with an island made of marble and stainless steel appliances.

As she cooked, Candy couldn't help but reminisce about her grandmother's words of wisdom, as she would stand next to her side, learning how to cook meals very much similar to the one she'd prepared today.

"Hand me some of that margarine out the icebox sweetie," Grandma said to a young Candy. She continued, "Ain't nothing like some sweet water cornbread made in an iron skillet on top of the stove. You see, we grease the skillet with cooking oil but once the cornbread is done you use the margarine to coat the cornbread with extra flava. Candy, you paying attention baby?"

"Yes ma'am," replied a young Candy.

"*Yo'* granddaddy *sho 'nuff* loved my cornbread. In fact after I fixed him a Sunday dinner with this sweet water cornbread I couldn't pay him to leave me alone," her grandmother said with a lighthearted laugh.

"So it's true, that a way to a man's heart is through his stomach, Grandma?" young Candy inquisitively asked.

"Well Baby, that's one way to lock him in. Every man enjoys a good home cooked meal. But I think that the way to truly have or earn a heart is loyalty. Every man wants a woman that's going to have their back, no matter what the circumstance. Just like I always had your granddaddy back. He knew that no matter what he did I was always going to be there to love and support and most importantly, have his best interest in mind. Loyalty is something that women now-a-day know nothing about. The first sign of rough times and these young *hoochies* off in *da* wind with the next Tom, Dick and Harry doing God knows what! A real man will always love and appreciate a loving, loyal woman, that is, if he was raised right."

Candy's trance was broken by the sound of the doorbell ringing as Jerome and Sapphire arrived. Before Candy could wash her hands, Snake emerged from the basement door.

"I got it Babe," he yells as he heads towards the front door and opens it.

"What's up Family?" he says blissfully as he offers to take their coats and place them on the coat rack. Warm welcoming hugs are given all around between the couples.

"Hey y'all! I'm glad you guys made it safely. Man, are the roads getting bad out there?" This Midwest snow ain't no joke!" states a jittery Candy.

"Yeah, I know. It just started coming down heavy out of nowhere," Jerome replies.

"It doesn't seem like it's sticking on the streets though, just on the grass and trees fo'real," adds a glowing Sapphire.

"You have a beautiful home Snake," continues Sapphire. "Thanks Sapphire or can I call you Lil Cuz now?" he jokingly asks.

"Lil Cuz will do just fine", Sapphire says as she eyes her beautiful engagement ring.

"Well, Lil Cuz it is then," a smiling Snake replies.

"Come on y'all. Let's chill in the living room while the potato salad chills in the fridge for about 10-15 minutes," announces Candy.

"Would y'all like a glass of wine or something stiffer?" asks Snake as the group moves to the living room.

"I'm cool with the wine, how about you Babe?" Jerome asks his lady.

"None for me Romey, I'm good," Sapphire says.

"What's up, you sick or something?" an interested Candy asks.

"Well, I'm not sick Candy, just expecting!" an exuberant Sapphire exclaims.

Jerome's eyes nearly pop out of his head as he jumps out of his seat and yells, "Baby you pregnant?"

"Yes Romey, you *gonna* be a daddy!" Sapphire responds with all smiles.

"Girl, when did you find out?" Candy inquisitively asks.

"I took a couple of home pregnancy tests today. I was going to wait until after dinner to make the announcement, but y'all didn't give me a chance," she divulges with a grin.

"Well, this is a cause for celebration fo'real!" Snake exclaims as he grabs three wine glasses and a bottle of apple juice for Sapphire.

"Girl, I am so happy for y'all! I'm *gonna* be an auntie! I'm going to be an auntie!" Candy playfully says as she dances in front of Sapphire.

"I'm *gonna* be a daddy!" a proud Jerome declares.

Snake uncorks the bottle of white wine and proposes a toast to Jerome and Sapphire, a.k.a "Lil Cuz". "May the new addition to the family be healthy, wealthy, wise and cute too," he finishes as the two couples chuckle and clink glasses.

After finishing their wine and bottle of apple juice respectively, the couples moved to the dining room to eat dinner. Snake and Jerome were impressed by Candy's cooking. Sapphire, privy to her best friend's culinary skills coupled with her newly found pregnancy state allowed her appetite free reign. She indulged accordingly!

Once the meal was over, the couples retreated to the comfort of the finished basement, which was equipped with a full wet bar, a 102 inch HD projection screen television, theater seating and a stage with stripper poles. Candy couldn't help but notice that Snake had put extra effort in setting the ambiance with French Vanilla candles lit throughout the basement, Jazz music lightly playing on the surround sound system, and two more bottles of white wine on ice sitting on the bar.

Candy, who was hesitant about exposing her and Sapphire's hand, was just about to spill the beans when Snake begin to speak. "This is a special day for more than one reason I hope," he says as he stands up while the other three remained seated. He continues, "With the new addition of the baby to our family, I want to make my own addition, if she'll have me!" Snake gets down on one knee in front of Candy. As he takes her hand and looks into her misty eyes, he proceeds. "Candy, ever since our first date Baby you've uniquely challenged and complemented me like no other woman I've met. You've become the cornerstone of my life and as my mother would say if she were here, I'd be a fool to let you go. Baby you make me a better man. You give me what I've been lacking as a man. You've given me the ability to love with the totality of my being and I never thought that would be possible for me. Candy Lanae' Sinclair will you do me the honor of becoming my wife, will you marry me?"

Both of Candy's hands held her sobbing face, pure joy and guilt overcame her emotionally, like a perfect storm. She struggled to regain her composure to be able to articulate her thoughts audibly.

She wiped her tears away and valiantly said, "Yes, I'll marry you."

They embraced and kissed passionately. Candy pulled away and looked Snake in his eyes, she mustarded up the courage to say, "Pernell Andre Collins, I have something I must tell you." She continued, "Baby, I love you with all my heart and you know that, but I have to tell you that our meeting wasn't by chance."

Snake stood there with a puzzled look on his face. What was supposed to be one of the happiest moments of his life had him feeling uneasy and suspicious.

"Baby, I need for you to hear me out before you interrupt or shut me out please?" she pleaded as Sapphire stood up by her side for support and in acknowledgement of her role in the plot. "Baby, it all stems from the reason why you're down here in Louisville in the first place," she exclaims.

Snake immediately goes on the defense with an animated facial expression. Jerome simultaneously becomes perturbed at hearing the statement regarding his cousin's relocation to Louisville. On several occasions his attempts to gain this information from Snake were put off; so now he would finally find out what prompted Snake's move.

"Baby, I know what kind of man you are and when you explained to me why you did what you did because of your mother's condition, I knew that my falling in love with you was no mistake. Sometimes what the enemy wants to use as your demise, God uses as your blessing."

"What is she talking about Cuz," Jerome interrupts.

"Let her finish Rome," Snake replies.

"Listen Baby, the guy who you told on has a Goon Squad. Do the names E-Tone and J.J. sound familiar?" Sapphire asked.

"Told on? What is she *talkin'* about cuz?" Jerome exclaims.

"Hold on Rome, I'll explain that later!" he says as he motions his cousin to sit down. "Yeah, I know about them," he finishes.

"Well Baby, we used to work for them," she says as she turns in Sapphire's direction. "Baby, if I didn't love you I would have never said a word about this and you know how this would have ended. But I genuinely fell deeply in love with you, please know that!"

Jerome interrupts again, "Sapphire, you was a part of this shit too?"

"Romey, let us finish explaining please," Sapphire pleads. Candy picks up her discourse.

"Baby, you already know how they get down and we can't just tell them that we're good on them or we've had a change of heart. They ain't going for that shit! If you don't kill them, then we're all up shit creck without a paddle!" Candy exclaims.

"Somebody tell me what the fuck is going on, seems like I'm the only one in the dark with this shit!" Jerome blurts out.

Sapphire intervenes, "Baby in a nutshell, we was sent down here to buddy up to your cousin because of something he did back home. Baby, I didn't know that I was going to meet you and fall in love with you, get married and have your baby, Romey. What we have is real Romey, not a *fuckin'* game!" Sapphire insists.

"What do they know so far and when was the last time you had contact with them?" Snake asked Candy.

"Cuz, what the fuck happened back in the Nati?" Jerome probes.

"Hold up Rome!" Snake fires back.

"I haven't talked to them in a few days, maybe close to a week or so now and you know if it was just about revenge with them you'd already be dead, but Baby they some money hungry, bloodthirsty ass niggas. They want to know where the money and the dope at, but I keep spinning they ass. Nell, I love you with all of my heart and I'm sorry to have met you under these circumstances, but it's too late for that now. I can't change my past or yours but we can take control of our future!" Sapphire says with sincerity.

"Look Rome, I fucked up! I got jammed up back in the city. It was when my Mama had been diagnosed with cancer and she had less than a year to live. I was caught between a rock and a hard place Fam. Either tell on my "*connect*" or miss out on the last few months of my Mama's life." Snake explains.

"You know we ain't been raised like that or built like that Cuz, but I understand. You know that them dudes was some heavy hitters, they wasn't *gonna* just let that shit slide," retorts Jerome.

"I know Cuz, I fucked up!" a dejected Snake says.

"Look Fam, we in this together. I got your back, regardless and since the girls told you the scoop, look like we all in this together. So what's the plan Cuz?" Jerome asks.

That day the sides had been chosen and the lines had been drawn. Candy and Sapphire had cleared the air about their mission of mayhem and mischief. They had made their beds and now it was time to lay in them. They had gambled with their hearts and now it was time to let the chips fall where they may.

Chapter 15

"West34! Your visitor is here," yells the C.O. in the A1 Housing Dormitory at Noble Correctional Center, where Vontez was serving time.

"Tez, I think they just called your bed number for your visit," Daryl says as he walks over to Vontez's bed area.

"Good looking out Homie," Vontez states as he finishes tying up his wheat colored Timberland boots.

"Who's coming to see you today?" asks Daryl.

"My dynamic duo!" replies Vontez as he exits the bed area and heads towards the C.O.'s desk to obtain his visitor's pass.

Once his pass is received, Vontez departs from the housing unit to the visiting room. While walking across the prison yard, Vontez observes the multitude of men on the pullup and dip bars, he thought to himself that if some of these guys put half as much effort into building up their minds as they put into building up their physique, they could collectively put a serious dent in the Ohio penal population.

Vontez reached the visiting room door and rang the buzzer. He patiently waited a couple of minutes before being let in by the visiting room porter. Once inside, Vontez handed the officer his pass and was escorted to a small room where he was strip searched before entering the visiting room. After gaining access to the visiting room, Vontez is greeted with wide smiles by both Keisha and Stephanie. After handing his identification badge to the guard at the visitor's office booth, Vontez is told to sit at table #12, where his two ladies awaited him, with radiant anticipation. As he gets closer to the table both ladies stand to greet their man. Stephanie being closest to Vontez is greeted first with an endearing hug and impassioned kisses, followed by Keisha. The C.O. and visitors alike, as always, were in awe of the happy trio, when Vontez was visited by his two women.

"Damn, y'all look good," Vontez remarks.

"That's you Baby! You got that glow and that blow!" Stephanie exclaims.

Keisha adds, "You *lookin'* like a male fitness model in here Tez. We *gonna* have to beat some hoes up about *yo'* ass when you come home *'cause* they *gonna* be all in *yo'* face," and they shared a laugh together.

"Y'all ain't got to worry about nobody else. I promise what we have is something special and I wouldn't do anything to fuck that up. Besides the way y'all put it on me, I ain't got the time, energy or desire for no one else, you feel me?" Vontez says enticingly.

"I know that's right. When you come home, we ain't going outside for weeks Tez! We got some serious making up to do Luv!" Keisha seductively states.

"We *gonna* drain *yo'* ass Boo! I think it's time for us to have some kids together... so you have to get on the job Baby *'cause* we both want to have *yo'* babies!" adds Stephanie.

"Oh yeah! Well, that ain't no problem ladies. I was hoping y'all would come to that conclusion. That's something I've been thinking about myself and speaking of kids, how are my kids doing?" inquires Vontez.

"They doing good *Bay*! Vonesha is so responsible and well mannered. Lashay is still shy as ever, but she's precious." states Keisha.

Stephanie continues, "Trinity is sweet too with her little cute self, but that little boy of yours is a mess."

"Whoa!" Vontez retorts.

"Yes, he is Tez! I mean he look just like you, but he shouldn't be acting like that at age 8 going on 9!" Keisha says as she picks up the conversation.

"More like 8 going on 19. Do you know what he said to us last time we saw him?" Stephanie poses the question to Vontez.

"No, what did he say Babe?" asked Tez. "This mannish little boy said that when he makes it to the NFL, that he's *gonna* have three girlfriends -- one chocolate, one brown skin and one redbone *'cause* he a boss like his daddy," Stephanie remarks in disbelief at the 8 year old's comments.

"Wow! Lil Tez is something else, I'm *gonna* have a talk with him. I'm going to try and call him when I get back in the block. Three girlfriends *doe*? He better make the league *'cause* if he don't, he *gonna* have to set them hoes on the track! Shit! That's an expensive dream right there." Vontez playfully says.

"Boy, you a mess! Set them hoes on the track *doe*? No wonder that boy act the way he act," Keisha says in fun.

"Yeah, he is most definitely his daddy's child. He gets it honest," Stephanie signifies.

"So what have you been up to Baby, besides working out?" asked Keisha.

"Well, to be honest, I've been reading a lot lately and you know I've been watching our show, 'Scandal'," Vontez remarked.

"That Kerry Washington is a bad chick, ain't she?" asked Stephanie rhetorically, not really expecting an answer from either of them.

"Now she can kick it wit us that one way, no questions asked! You feel me!" Keisha chimes in.

"You know it girl! I still can't believe that Olivia's dad had Harrison killed and she don't even know it yet," Stephanie adds.

"Yeah that threw me for a loop too!" Tez utters.

"He definitely can't be trusted." Keisha persists.

The unconventional lovers continue their small talk for a few hours, while enjoying each other's company during the visit.

"Baby, we have some very good news that we've been saving. We didn't want you to try and talk us out of it! We want to leave you with something to ponder," Keisha states.

Stephanie picks up the conversation where Keisha left off, "You're already going to be on 5 years paper because you got an F1, so we talked to the lawyer about filing for a judicial release for you. We should know something in the next 30 days!"

"Wow, I don't know what to say," Vontez stammers.

"You don't have to say *nothin'* Papi. Just keep your fingers crossed," Keisha adds.

The pair said their goodbyes accompanied with long goodbye kisses and the girls made their way to the visiting room exit door. Vontez watched them switch and sashay seductively until out of view.

Again Vontez is strip searched when leaving the visiting room building. He reflects on the situation that was presented to him by his two women. As he walks back across the yard to his dorm he thinks about all of the things that he has tried to block out on a daily basis. Things like being able to take and pick up his children to and from school, being able to attend Tez's football games next season, being able to spend time with his mother and brother without the supervision of correctional officers hovering around them. And being able to enjoy the warmth and comfort of his own home and his women. He was most definitely pondering the thought of getting his freedom and life back in all facets.

Chapter 16

"Daddy why did LeBron James go to Cleveland? He should have stayed with Bosch and Wade and won another championship in Miami, I'm salty!" says Little Eric.

"He went to Cleveland because that's the team he used to play for, before going to Miami. And, in case you didn't know it, LeBron is from Ohio, just like you," E-Tone tells his son.

"What? I didn't know that Daddy. That must have been in the old days huh?" Eric says.

"Well, it wasn't that long ago, only 4 years but you were only 3 years old so I don't think you remember," E-Tone tells his son with a chuckle.

"So can we go to a basketball game this year Daddy and see LeBron?" Little Eric asks his father.

"I think I can make that happen for you son as long as you don't get into any trouble at school and you keep your grades up. Is that a deal?" E-Tone asked his son.

"Yes sir!" an excited Little Eric replies to his dad.

"Eric!" yells his wife Samantha.

"Yes Babe?" he replies.

"Can you come in here please?" she asks her husband.

"Where you at Babe?" he responds.

"In the laundry room," Samantha retorts.

After making his way down the stairs to the laundry room, E-Tone enters to find his wife holding up a pair of blood stained black sweat pants and matching blood soaked sweat suit jacket.

"Listen Eric, we've already talked about this. I know that you're still in the streets, but you promised me that you wouldn't bring that life to our house. E.J. and I don't deserve that life and I won't accept it! Why would you bring this shit back here where you live? Either you getting too comfortable with mess or *yo'* ass is getting sloppy!" Samantha fires her comments at E-Tone like armor piercing bullets from his own personal collection.

"Babe, I'm sorry. It won't happen again I promise! But you know that's my favorite Jordan sweat suit," he says arrogantly and with sarcasm.

"Boy bye! You act like you broke or something. Next time throw that shit away! And the shoes too!" she screams.

"Ok, ok Babe I will! I promise!" he says more sincerely this time. He continues, "Speaking of business Babe, I gotta go out of town for a few days, I'll be back this weekend."

"Well, ok. Are you *gonna* give me some money to finish Christmas shopping or what?" Samantha asserts.

"How much do you need?"

"About this much," she answers as she gestures the size of the stack of money with her hands.

After satisfying his wife's request and saying goodbye to his 7 year old son, E-Tone leaves the comfort of his suburban Cincinnati home to enter into the erratic environment of the streets. Once inside the tinted out Lincoln MKZ, E-Tone calls his partner in crime.

"Whose pussy is this? Whose pussy is this huh?" J.J. forcefully asks Peaches.

"It's yours Daddy! Damn you fuck me so good!" she exclaims in ecstasy as J.J.'s phone rings.

The distinctive ringtone of B-Legits "Playa Partners" alerts J.J. that it's his homeboy E-Tone on the other end. While in mid-stroke, he answers the call.

"What's good Homie?"

"You! Are you ready to hit the road, my guy?" E-Tone asks.

"Yeah, *gimme* about 20 minutes."

"Damn that dick feels good Daddy!!!" Peaches hollers out in the background.

"Make that a half hour Homie," J.J. finishes.

"You over Peaches' crib?" E-Tone poses the question.

"You already know," replies J.J.

"I'm on my way," E-Tone says with a light chuckle.

Taking the scenic route, E-Tone arrives in Bond Hill, at Peaches' house a half hour later to pick up J.J. He blows the horn and J.J. appears in the doorway with a scantily dressed Peaches draped all over him. He reluctantly pulls himself away from the desirable vixen and makes his way to the awaiting vehicle.

"What up with it Homeboy?" a smiling J.J. says as he enters the vehicle.

"Looks like you and Ole Girl are what's up my G," a smirking E-Tone replies.

"Yeah, she can't get enough of *yo'* boy! I think I might put a baby in her fine ass, just to lock her in that one way! Damn, did I just say that shit out loud?" a giddy J.J. asks rhetorically.

"Hell yeah, you did. She got that ass whipped like butter Homie!" E-Tone jokes with his partner in crime and the two men share a good laugh.

129

"Serious business though. These hoes ain't even been answering the phone lately. Bitches keep texting me back, talkin bout they still on the case and shit!" an increasingly agitated E-Tone expresses.

"Well let's pay 'em an unexpected visit then Homie! So we can see what it is for ourselves then!" exclaims J.J.

"You already know! I'm *gonna* stop down at Thornton's to grab some coffee for the road," E-Tone states.

"Sounds like a plan to me," says J.J.

Meanwhile it had been a week since Candy and Sapphire had reluctantly revealed their participation in the plot against their fiancés. Happy to finally have that heavy burden of betrayal off of their chest, the girls were at their condo, busily packing up belongings, to move in with their respective future husbands.

"I'm so happy that this mess is almost over with. I don't want my baby growing up in this crazy lifestyle we've been a part of," states Sapphire.

"It ain't quite over yet. The tough part has only begun fo'real. Snake said he has a plan and to stall E-Tone and J.J. until after Christmas, so that's what we gotta do. So, don't take everything out of your closet, in case they pop up on us. We don't want them to suspect anything, especially considering the position we're in now," says Candy.

"Yes, since it's evident that we are both in love with the enemy! You know I just feel bad for Romey. You *gotta* understand his position, he was blind-sided by this whole

130

thing, and I thought Snake had filled him in on why he relocated. But I guess not. Jerome knows that I'm in love with him. I just have to give him a chance to come around. Besides now we're all in this together," commented a disheartened Sapphire.

"What does Snake have up his sleeve? Are we all going to relocate or something? *'Cause* you know it's not going to be that easy, them dudes got eyes and ears everywhere!" Sapphire declares.

"I don't know yet. But he said he's got it covered and I believe in him. He knows that we got just as much to lose as him-- our lives!" she asserts.

The two women continued to gather up clothes and other belongings over the next hour or so, packing the items into plastic bins, to take to their new living quarters. Candy took some items down to her car, which was parked in the rear parking lot of the building. She didn't notice the Black Lincoln with the tinted windows parked next to her as she loaded the bins in her trunk.

"What's up Candy-Cane, you going on a trip or something Boo?" E-Tone says as he rolls down the tinted windows revealing his identity to Candy.

"Damn, you scared the shit out of me!" she yells as she is startled by E-Tone's appearance.

"What you scared of Candy-Cane? You got that look on *yo'* face, like *yo'* Mama just caught you doing something you ain't supposed to be doing. Are you?" he teasingly asked.

"Naw, boy please! Go on with that shit! What up though! Why you *poppin'* up and shit? I told you I was still working on it. You act like you don't trust my judgement no more," she fires at E-Tone.

"Well, you *actin'* like that dick *cloudin' yo'* judgment, *'cause* this shit should've been wrapped up! Fuck all this parking lot pimpin', let's talk upstairs," he yells back, as he and J.J. exit the vehicle. After closing the trunk Candy has her qualms about going upstairs, but reluctantly obliges. Luckily, Sapphire observed the exchange in the parking lot, from her bedroom window. She quickly slides the plastic bins from the living room into their bedroom closets, so the men wouldn't see them, confirming their suspicion.

Once inside the privacy of the condo, E-Tone interrogates Candy and Sapphire about their focus and loyalties. After unimpressively arguing their point of view, Candy and Sapphire are given an ultimatum of getting the information needed to wrap up this mission or "go down with the ship" was the phrase E-Tone used to instill an already hovering fear in the women.

Chapter 17

Christmas was just over a week away and Verdale was shoveling his driveway and the sidewalk in front of his newly built home, located in Wyoming, a quiet suburb right on the outside of Cincinnati. After completing the chore, Verdale applied salt to the freshly shoveled areas and put the shovel and the bag of salt in the garage. Opening the door in the garage that led to the side kitchen entrance, he is greeted by an aromatic blend of hot cocoa and chocolate chip cookies.

"Sit your handsome, hardworking-self right down and get warm baby," orders Gina. "I made two of your favorites, hot cocoa with extra marshmallows and walnut chocolate chip cookies. Crunchy just the way you like 'em Babe."

"Girl, I love *yo'* thoughtful ass!" he bellows in an animated fashion causing his wife to laugh.

"Dale you turn into a big kid when I make your favorite and I love it," she announces as his cell phone rings.

"Hey Ma! What's up beautiful?" declares Verdale as he answers his phone.

"Hey son, what are you doing in about an hour when I get off work?"

"I'll probably be at your house shoveling your driveway and sidewalk still, why? What's up Ma? Is something wrong?" He asks his mother.

"Well, not exactly Dale, but you know how I am about my dreams and I keep having the same dream. I'll see you when I get home and I love you son," she says before ending the phone call.

"I love you too Ma." Dale replies as he hangs up the phone.

"Is Mama V alright?" asked Regina.

"Yeah, she said something about having a reoccurring dream, I guess about me, I'm assuming. After I finish this hot cocoa and cookies, I'm *gonna* head over there and get her driveway cleared. I'll talk to her more about it then," he says to his concerned wife.

"Your Mama got a gift with her dreams. Remember she kept dreaming about Tez getting bit by a snake before he caught his case. And that wasn't a coincidence at all," she declares.

"I know, I know," a mildly irritated Dale responds. "Well, let's just hope her skills of intuition are on the fritz."

After finishing his snack, Dale heads over to his mother's house. The snowfall at her house was much less than at his own house so it didn't take long at all to clear and salt her driveway and sidewalk. Right on schedule as he is putting away the tools and supplies, his mother pulls up.

As she gets out the car she says, "Brrr!! It's getting' cold out here. Hey Babyboy, thanks for getting me together. You know how I hate raking leaves, cutting grass and shoveling snow. I don't think your Mama was cut out for yard work, that's why God gave me two sons."

"God knew what he was doing Mama, I'm done in here. You want me to pull the Cadi in the garage before I come in?" Verdale asked his mother.

"Thanks Baby, if you don't mind," she replies as she tosses him the keys.

Mama V unlocks the door to the house from the garage and enters. Verdale enters the house a moment later after moving the SUV into the garage and closing it. Mama V was washing her hands in the kitchen sink and reached in the cabinet to grab two coffee mugs, one for her and one for her youngest son. She rinsed the mugs out in the sink before grabbing the Swiss Miss hot chocolate box from the pantry. Observing his mother preparing his favorite hot beverage, Verdale initiates the dialogue.

"So what's up Ma, with this dream you keep having? It must be about me huh?" he asked his mother.

"Well, yeah. You know how I am. I always felt bad about not telling your brother the dreams about him *gettin'* bit by a snake, before he got jammed up. That dream was just like the one I had about your daddy, riding in an ambulance before he was shot and killed. My mother used to have dreams about things before they happened just like her mother had them before her. I don't know if it's a family gift or a curse. But at any rate, I have it now. I keep having the same dream about somebody following you. Every dream, it's somebody different following you, but you never see them. Their faces are blurry so I can't tell you what they look like, but I can say for sho' that they didn't mean you no good, Baby Boy! I can't exactly interpret the dream, but I do know that when I wake up from these dreams I have the same feeling of uneasiness that I had with your father and your brother!"

Valencia retrieves the two mugs of hot chocolatey pleasure from the microwave. She then removes a bag of mini marshmallows from the pantry and places them, along with the cup of cocoa in front of her son. She sits down at the kitchen table with her youngest offspring and removes a small bag of marijuana and rolling papers from a porcelain fixture on the table. She effortlessly twists up a joint and sparks it up.

"See this mess got my nerves all bad and shit son," she says.

Verdale chuckles slightly and says to his now more relaxed mother, "what do you think I should do Ma, hire a bodyguard or something?"

"I don't know Dale but you do have Gina and the twins to worry about. I would stay on my P's and Q's. Just be more aware of your surroundings from now on. *I'ma* talk to your brother about y'all doing something different with y'all lives. It's time for a change. I've turned a blind eye to y'all dealing escapades because I knew that y'all could handle y'all selves and I selfishly enjoyed the perks, I am ashamed to say. But y'all comfortable now. It's time to take that money and do something different. Hell, both y'all already got businesses that make money now. I know not like the game, but still y'all already good," his mother says as she takes another puff of the relaxing reefer stick.

"Ma, it's not that easy. We got too many people, and too many families depending on us to just quit. It's not as simple as you're making it," Verdale responds to his mother's plea.

"You mean to tell me that those people and their families are more important than your own?" she yells back at him before taking another draw of the *wacky tobacky.*

"Naw Ma. I'm not saying that at all but we got people depending on us to feed their families, so we can't just quit supplying them cold turkey. We have to prepare them for the transition," Dale explains.

"See you *talkin'* to me like you in a business meeting. I ain't one of your God-damn flunkies Dale! I'm *yo'* Mama and I don't give a fuck about those other folks, all I care about is you and *yo'* brother. We need y'all to be smart and not greedy. What come up must come down. You know the game don't last forever! Hell even I know that is one of the most important rules in the game; besides not getting high on your own supply!" Valencia badgers her son before ashing the cannabis cigarette.

"Ma, with all due respect you're right, but this is something that me and Tez need to talk about. Not you and me. I can't shut down something that I volunteered to maintain for him, without consulting him first. Ma, I hope you understand, and I will be extra cautious from now on. I promise. I don't want you to worry Ma, I got this fo'real," Verdale attempts to reassure a concerned Valencia.

"You got this? Ok, I'm *gonna* leave it alone, son. I've spoken my peace on the matter and that is all I can do." Mama V concedes.

The mother and son finish their warm drinks and change the subject to solidifying their holiday plans. Verdale leaves his mother's house with a renewed awareness of his surroundings.

Chapter 18

It was Christmas Eve, and the whole crew was at the "Snake Pit" having a private Christmas Party for staff and family only. "This Christmas" by the Whispers was playing over the sound system, which Monique the bartender had setup using her iPad. Snake and Jerome slipped away from the party-goers to talk in the back office.

"Cuz have you decided how you want to handle this yet? Sapphire's been *stressin'* over this shit and stress ain't good for her or the baby. So, we got to either handle this shit head on or either get the fuck out of town," a liquor relaxed Jerome reiterated to his cousin.

"Yeah, I got something figured out. Candy and I have been discussing some scenarios and I think we got something to trip up these goofy goon ass niggas." Snake informs his cousin.

After briefing Jerome on the particulars of his strategy, they return to the bar area from the privacy of the rear office. Everyone was in a merry, festive party mode with spiked egg nog and hard apple cider flowing freely throughout the bar. Due to her pregnancy, Sapphire was drinking cranberry juice.

Their Secret Santa gift exchange was a success, with everyone completely satisfied with their gifts. The entire staff had their significant other with them, including Luke who had brought Tiffany, the young lady he had met at the bar a couple of months earlier (the one with the stalker for an ex-boyfriend). Tiny brought his baby Mama, Clairissa. Precious had brought her most recent love interest Mario, who she met while he was delivering liquor to the bar. Monique brought her kids' father, Terrence, to the party. The barmaids and the other security personnel were also there with their respective partners.

The Charles Brown classic, "Please Come Home for Christmas", began playing over the sound system. All the couples took advantage of the classic holiday love song and headed for the dance floor to slow dance.

Snake and Candy were dancing just like the other couples when Candy addressed her fiancé, "Pernell Andre Collins, I love you with all my heart."

"I love you too, Candy Lanae' Sinclair," Snake replies.

"Baby for the first time in my life I truly am happy. All of my loyalties belong to you and only you. And no matter how this situation plays out, I want you to know that," Candy expresses to Snake.

"Baby although the way we met may have been less than favorable on my part, I wouldn't change a thing about it. You know everything about me. The good, the bad and the embarrassing, and with you I don't have to try to be someone I'm not. All of my cards are on the table and I know that together we can make this a winning hand," Snake tells Candy as he lightly embraces her while they continue to move in unison to the music.

After the slow dancing ended the group converged on the catered soul food buffet prepared by Alabama Que BBQ Restaurant, provided at Snake's expense. To get everyone's attention, Jerome hits his fork against his glass, signaling for quiet. After gaining everyone's attention, he begins sharing his appreciation for those present.

"First of all I want to thank everyone for attending our first annual Christmas party at the Snake Pit." The crowd breaks into applause. "And of course this wouldn't be possible without my cousin, best friend and partner Snake." He continues after another round of applause, "I want to thank every staff member on behalf of my cousin and myself for making this first year of business a complete success." These comments were followed by another round of applause.

141

"Everyone here has played a part in our collective success and made us the hottest club in the city!"

The staff bursts out in cheers. While his cousin Jerome continues his announcements, Snake rises to stand by his side holding a hand full of envelopes.

Jerome then says, "and for that we are grateful! To show our appreciation with more than just words, it's Christmas bonus time!"

"Now that's what I'm talking about," an animated Luke chimes in.

The co-workers, staff and family members laugh, as Snake proceeds to pass out envelopes filled with five brand new one hundred dollar bills to the valued employees of the Snake Pit. Everyone was happy and surprised to receive a bonus. The party which started at 5p.m. continued until around 9p.m. with the staff members all chipping in to clean up before dispersing to their own individual homes to prepare for the holiday the following morning.

Meanwhile...

Christmas Eve in the joint was like <u>Ground Hog Day</u>, the movie, for Vontez. It was business as usual with the exception of a Christmas program being held in the chapel. Vontez, although he was raised in church and believed in God, didn't normally attend the church services in the penitentiary, due to the lack luster spirit of the men who attended and because of the *Gumps* who would choose to use the chapel as a meeting spot. However Vontez was compelled to go to the holiday service this Christmas Eve. Maybe it was because he missed his children and other family members so much. Or was it the overwhelming need he felt to pray regarding his judicial release being in limbo. Or maybe it was something in his spirit that strongly encouraged, almost coerced him to attend.

Whatever the reason, when the yard opened after chow, Vontez made his way to the chapel. Upon entering the chapel, Vontez was greeted by outside guests who were shaking the hands of inmates as they entered the facility. Once seated, the prison band and choir began to play and sing Christmas songs, creating a very lively and festive atmosphere. The resident chaplain, Chaplain Benton Rose, took the podium and said a few words before handing over the program to the guest speaker, Dwayne Abernathey.

"To God be the glory, he began. I know it is Christmas time and you all are used to hearing about the birth of Christ. Every Christmas service, just like clockwork, Amen! I wanted to talk to you today about purpose, specifically about your purpose in life. The Bible says in Mark 10:45, *"for even the son of man, did not come to be served, but to serve and to give his life as a ransom for many."*

You see at this time of year we celebrate the beginning of a predestined process of which the completion meant Christ's death, as a sacrifice for all man-kind, by dying on that cross at Calvary. Jesus fulfilled his purpose on this earth. Are you walking in your destiny? Can I get an Amen somebody!

I know that because of your current location, you may be confused about what God has called you to do. Confused about what your purpose in life truly is, can I get an Amen somebody! Well, I'm here to tell you that God has a purpose for each and every one of you under the sound of my voice. The catch is, just like he gives us free will about what direction we want to take our lives, you also have free will to find out what your own true purpose is in life and it doesn't matter that you are in a place full of rules, limitations and restrictions because you still have the free will to decide which direction you want to take.

The Bible says in Luke 12:48 *"to whom much is given, much is required."* Many of you have been given talents that the average man would envy, but you haven't chosen to use them properly or have taken them for granted because they come so effortlessly to you. Can I get an Amen somebody?"

The crowd responds with a rumble of Amens.

"Some of the most talented, productive and successful people in society have served time in prison. The only difference between you and them........ he paused for dramatic effect, is they made a conscious decision to walk in their purpose. Comedian Tim Allen, from the hit TV series Home Improvement, served time in a federal penitentiary. Don King, the boxing promoter, served time in an Ohio prison before going on to be one of, if not the most successful and well known boxing promoters in recent history. Lyfe

Jennings served time in another Ohio correctional facility, where he discovered and honed his love and incredible talent for music. Once released, he stayed focused and pursued his dreams of a music career. I give you these tangible examples of men of success that were incarcerated. You have all heard of them and the only difference between you and them is, walking in your purpose. Can I get an Amen somebody?"

A more hyped-up crowd responds, more lively with a barrage of Amens, including Vontez.

"Some of you have a natural ability to be a leader; people just seem to gravitate to you like bees to honey. Use that natural leadership ability to steer some people in the right direction. Become a career counselor or a life coach. Some of you have been hooked on drugs, but through the grace of God you've been able to kick that habit. Share the benefits of your knowledge and firsthand experience to become a drug counselor to help others escape the stronghold of addiction. Some of you work out so much that you look like modern day superheroes." The crowd laughs at his observation. "Get certified, become a nutritionist and personal trainer. Walk into your purpose! Can I get an Amen somebody?"

Now the crowd is really amped up and he gets some of the men on their feet as they shout Amen, including Vontez.

"The artists, musicians, authors and poets that are sitting before me, I urge you to use your God-given abilities to create and sustain a profitable income and outlet for your talents once your liberation from the system comes. If you can eat off of your talents in here, then you will strive and thrive in the free world. I can assure you of that. But you have to have a plan, stay focused and most importantly walk into the purpose of which God has already set for your life. "

The motivational speaker spoke for a few more minutes before the choir and band ministered again. Chaplain Benton said a few closing remarks but repeated the theme of the speaker. Dwayne Abernathey's message seemed to echo in Vontez's mind as he left the service and walked back across the prison yard to his dormitory. He thought to himself, am I walking in my purpose?

Chapter 19

Christmas had been a time for E-Tone and J.J. to spend time with their families, escaping the tensions of their chosen profession. Monday December 29, 2014, E-Tone received a text message from Candy saying, "It's going down today, call me when you get up!" E-Tone looked at his phone and smiled his sinister grin, as he anticipated the very lucrative conclusion to a lengthy and costly scheme.

He wiped the sleep out of his eyes and rolled back over away from the nightstand toward his wife. "Good morning Beautiful!" he says to his wife, as he kissed her gently on the forehead.

"I see someone woke up in a good mood," Samantha says playfully to her affectionate spouse.

"Today is going to be the day for finishing up some shit!" E-Tone explains to his wife.

"Keep me out of the loop on that mess! You just be safe Eric," she replies.

"Don't worry Babe, I got this!" E-Tone responds. After brushing his teeth and washing his face, E-Tone returns Candy's text with a phone call; she answers the phone.

"What's up Candy-Cane?" he greets his accomplice.

"Did you get my message?"

"Yeah, I got it. What's going down?" he questions Candy.

"I got him to let me ride with him today when he re-ups. He said he needed someone that he could trust to know how to handle shit in case something happens to him, I guess putting Sapphire on his cousin worked like a charm. Especially since he made the comment that his cousin was too preoccupied with ole girl to focus on business," she informs E-Tone.

"Ok den, look like you been on the job as always. My bad for questioning your loyalties. But I had to put a fire up under *yo'* ass just to keep you focused on the job at hand, but it's all good. So, you know where he keeps the money and the dope?" he inquires of Candy.

"Well see that's the beauty of everything. He's going to re-up and he only re-ups three times a year, so it's going to be a boat load of shit. So I figured you could *lay down* him and *"the connect"* and get the money and the dope," says Candy. Her words were like music to his ears.

"Well if it's that much shit it's *gonna* be some muscle around or some *muthafuckas* to load that shit up or something?" E-Tone interrogates Candy.

"I already asked that shit. I told him that I didn't want to go if it's *gonna* be like a movie drug deal with goons standing around with guns and briefcases and shit. But he told me that it's always just him and *"the connect"* in an abandoned warehouse and that he has a false floor in his truck to store the dope. As a matter of fact, me being there is going to be a surprise to *"the connect"*. Anyway he's coming to pick me up around noon. You and J.J. need to be somewhere close by where y'all can follow us out to the spot, *'cause* I don't have an address to give y'all," she instructs E-Tone.

"Alright. We'll be within close range. Keep your phone on in case we lag too far behind. You can let us know what exit to take or whatever," he tells Candy.

"Alright, it's on!" She replies as they end the phone call.

Feeling good about the information he just received, E-Tone call his partner in crime, J.J.

"What's up Homie?" J.J. answers.

"It's time for the *"shotty"*, you feel me," E-Tone says, referring to J.J.'s trusty shotgun.

"Oh, word?" J.J. responds.

"Yep, Yep," E-Tone retorted.

"Okay den! Well, you know where I'm at," says J.J.

"Get ready, *'cause* I'm on the way," E-Tone instructs.

After picking up J.J. from Peaches' house and on their way to Louisville, E-Tone brings him up to speed. Arriving with a half hour to spare the pair decide to do their own pre-robbery investigation. They position themselves outside of Snake's gated community, inconspicuously enough not to be noticed, but in close enough range to see him exiting the secured gates. Within 20 minutes of posting up they follow him to Candy's crib without being noticed. They continue to follow Snake, who is now accompanied by Candy to I-75 north. Once on the expressway they continue to observe the charcoal gray Range Rover from a safe and clear distance. As they approach the exit ramp for the state route road, they speed up slightly as not to miss the direction of their turn.

They were just in time to see the Range Rover's right blinker flash, as the vehicle turns right. E-Tone follows the SUV, another two miles on the state route before it makes a left turn onto what looked like an old industrial road with several abandoned warehouses and factories. Before making the same left turn the pair of larcenist observe which warehouse the Range Rover disappears into.

The two men park their vehicle in the back of the first warehouse in the industrial park. E-Tone grabs his two 40cal handguns and a back pack full of zip ties, rope and a bag of rags. J.J., equipped with his trusty shotgun, also carried a 9mm as his back-up weapon. He made his way to the rear of the warehouse, as E-Tone positioned himself to enter from

150

the front. They listen from both their vantage points to the conversations inside.

"What's up O.G.?" says Snake as he exits the Range Rover and extends his hand to Agent Erkenburger, who was dressed in regular street clothes.

"What's up Snake? Who the dame with ya?" asked Guy, referring to Candy's presence at their meeting.

"My apologies O.G. This is my girl Candy."

"Oh, now that we got the introductions out the way, what the fuck is she doing here?" he yells at Snake.

"Man, she's good. I'm just showing her the ropes in case I become indisposed. You feel me?" Snake replies defensively.

"You should have let me know first. We've been doing business too long for any surprises now. You know I don't like surprises. But I'll take your word on her. What happened to that cousin of yours, who you were grooming? I'd think you would've brought him instead of this young woman," Guy poses the question and awaits a response from Snake.

"Plans change! Anyway he's focusing his attention elsewhere right now and I think she has the mindset for this. You feel me?" responds Snake.

E-Tone couldn't help but chuckle at the comments made about Candy because he knew she was a thoroughbred and built more for the game than what they knew. He was sitting back, waiting for the signal that he and J.J. had agreed upon, which was the point of exchange. That moment when the money and the dope would both be exposed.

"Well if you say so. Like we old timers say if you like it, then I love it," replies Guy. "It's a pleasure to meet you young lady," he addresses Candy. She extends her hands and he kisses it as a sign of chivalry.

"The pleasure is all mine. I've heard so much about you," Candy coyly replies.

"Oh have you? Let's hope it was all good things," Guy says flirtatiously.

Snake smiles at the suave façade of his supplier before breaking the awkwardness of the moment by saying, "let's make this short and sweet if you don't mind."

Snake pops the rear hatch on the Range Rover. He lifts the carpet floor at the corners and where the spare tire should be located reveals a black duffel bag full of cash. He pulls out the bag and Agent Erkenburger pops the trunk of his vehicle. He directs Snake to put the bag in his trunk and remove the 3 duffel bags full of product from his trunk. Just as Snake is about to make the exchange, E-Tone emerges from the shadows with both 40 caliber guns in hand looking like a black Yosemite Sam.

"Hold it right there!" he yells as he gestures for Snake to step away from the vehicle. Just as Snake flinches like he's going for something, J.J. steps out the darkness from the rear and cocks his shotgun.

"Not so fast Homeboy!" J.J. shouts to a stunned Snake.

"What the fuck is this?" Agent Erkenburger hollers out. "I knew this young bitch was bad news!" he continues in frustration.

"Shut the fuck up old man!" Candy snaps, mugging the agent in the face.

"Damn Babe! You on that? I thought you was my ride or die! Fake ass bitch!" Snake snarls in anger.

"Fuck you, you snitching-ass fuck boy!" Candy says as she stands side-by-side with E-Tone.

"Yeah *muthafucka*. It's time to pay the piper! Now turn y'all ass around, noses against the *fuckin'* truck!" E-Tone commands of Snake and Guy. "Get those zip ties out the backpack and secure their hands." E-Tone orders Candy. While Candy zip ties the two men, E-Tone directs J.J. to grab the 4 duffel bags.

Agent Erkenburger screams out, "Do y'all know who you *fuckin'* wit?" Before E-Tone or J.J. could answer, ATF agents rush into the warehouse after hearing the signal phrase uttered from Guy's mouth.

"Freeze!" yells the lead officer, startling E-Tone who fires a shot in the direction of the first ATF agent in his view.

Several agents return fire, striking E-Tone in the chest and stomach. J.J.'s shotgun was by his leg propped up against the agent's car. As he was removing the duffel bags, he squats down and grabs the shotgun, squeezing off two shots striking one of the ATF agents in the face. His comrades immediately return fire striking J.J. in the shoulder, the upper chest and a bullet grazes his head splitting his ear. He screams in pain as blood gushes down the side of his face.

One of the agents yell, "give it up James Jones, you're surrounded".

J.J.'s life flashed before his eyes, the gruesome murders, the large amounts of cash and dope he had taken and enjoyed. The fancy cars and fine women he had fucked. Peaches' face and beautiful smile saturated his mind. He thought if they knew his name and if he had killed one of their agents, he was never going to enjoy the comforts and amenities of freedom again.

Realizing this, J.J. decides his own fate. He raises his shotgun and manages to get off three more shots, connecting on two of them. He is struck repeatedly by a barrage of bullets from the agents. Agent Erkenburger emerges from behind the Range Rover where he and Snake had taken cover.

"Get these zip ties off of me!" he shouts to one of the other agents. "You alright Snake?" he asks.

A relieved Snake smiles as he sees his future wife unharmed. "Yeah, I'm good. It took y'all long enough to get in this *muthafucka*! Damn, Babe you were convincing as fuck!" Snake says to a visibly shaken Candy.

While the agents cut the zip ties that bound his hands, he immediately grabs and comforts a frazzled and crying Candy. She manages to say, "If you check their weapons," referring to E-Tone and J.J., "you'll solve at least 10 unsolved homicides in the tristate area."

"Hey! This one's not dead!" one of the ATF agents blurts out as he kicks the 40 caliber weapons away from E-Tone's blood stained body.

"Yeah, he's still breathing!" the agent continues.

"Good, let's get a bus in here! Somebody call for an ambulance. We can save his ass, then lock him up for life!" Guy yells to no one in particular.

As the lead agent stands over E-Tone, who is clinging to life he states, "Thanks for the tip, Agent Erkenburger. We've been trying to find something concrete on these guys for years, but they were the real deal. They left little for us to go on, but thanks to the tip from this young lady and Snake here, maybe the folks in the Tri-State area can sleep a little easier!" the lead ATF Agent commented.

"Now, how's the agent who was shot," asked Guy?

"We lost one, the others had their vests on and luckily they took shots to the body," replied the lead ATF agent.

The fake money and dope, in the duffel bags were taken by the ATF agents and the crime scene was secured to be thoroughly investigated. The couple who was still shaken but overcome with relief continued to embrace and comfort each other. E-Tone was placed in the ambulance. As the ambulance doors closed, his eyes opened just in time to see Candy being held in Snake's arms.

Chapter 20

Tuesday, December 30, 2014 Verdale is seated on his plush, comfy recliner in the basement of his regal home, in the comfort of his man cave flicking through the channels on the TV, when he comes across a "CNN" news bulletin.

"Two of the Midwest's most vicious and brutal killers are off the streets. One dead and one clinging to life after being shot in an exchange of gunfire with the ATF as they were cornered and eventually apprehended. James Jones, 32 years of age and Eric Carter, 33 years of age both from the Cincinnati Tri-State area," the news reporter says as their mugshots pop up. "They were suspects in at least 10 unsolved murders dating back to the year 2000," the reporter continues.

"Jones was killed during the violent exchange of gunfire. Carter is in critical condition but doctors are optimistic that he will survive to face the charges against him. Regional Narcotics Agent Guy Erkenburger is credited with giving the ATF the information leading to the capture and unfortunate death of one of the two murder suspects. More on this story on our 6 o'clock broadcast," the news correspondent says before the regularly scheduled program returned.

Verdale couldn't believe it – hearing the news regarding his hitmen. He couldn't help but wonder if Snake had something to do with the demise of his goons. He thought he recognized the name Guy Erkenburger as the arresting officer in his brother's case. In need of a drink to calm his nerves, Verdale tells Gina that he is going to the liquor store and will be right back. He hops in his Escalade, still in shock. Verdale doesn't notice the black Ford F-150 with tinted windows following him as he gets on the interstate.

To Be Continued!!!!!

Printed in Dunstable, United Kingdom